Tech Leadership Playbook

Building and Sustaining High-Impact Technology Teams

Alexsandro Souza

Apress®

Tech Leadership Playbook: Building and Sustaining High-Impact Technology Teams

Alexsandro Souza
Dublin, County Dublin, Ireland

ISBN-13 (pbk): 979-8-8688-0542-4   ISBN-13 (electronic): 979-8-8688-0543-1
https://doi.org/10.1007/979-8-8688-0543-1

Managing Director, Apress Media LLC: Welmoed Spahr
Acquisitions Editor: Shivangi Ramachandran
Development Editor: James Markham
Editorial Project Manager: Jessica Vakili

Cover designed by eStudio Calamar

Distributed to the book trade worldwide by Springer Science+Business Media New York, 1 New York Plaza, Suite 4600, New York, NY 10004-1562, USA. Phone 1-800-SPRINGER, fax (201) 348-4505, e-mail orders-ny@springer-sbm.com, or visit www.springeronline.com. Apress Media, LLC is a California LLC and the sole member (owner) is Springer Science + Business Media Finance Inc (SSBM Finance Inc). SSBM Finance Inc is a **Delaware** corporation.

For information on translations, please e-mail booktranslations@springernature.com; for reprint, paperback, or audio rights, please e-mail bookpermissions@springernature.com.

Apress titles may be purchased in bulk for academic, corporate, or promotional use. eBook versions and licenses are also available for most titles. For more information, reference our Print and eBook Bulk Sales web page at http://www.apress.com/bulk-sales.

Any source code or other supplementary material referenced by the author in this book is available to readers on GitHub. For more detailed information, please visit https://www.apress.com/gp/services/source-code.

If disposing of this product, please recycle the paper

Table of Contents

About the Author

 **Alexsandro Souza** is a writer, instructor, and open source contributor. With over 14 years of experience in the software development industry, he has been employed by companies worldwide, during which he led many teams on a variety of projects.

With a diverse background encompassing backend and frontend development, DevOps, microservices, big data, computer vision, deep learning, team leadership, and project management, his expertise is both extensive and profound, enabling a holistic approach to technology solutions that fuel innovation and growth.

In addition to his professional achievements, he is dedicated to making a positive impact on the community by creating and sharing articles, videos, lectures, and educational courses on Udemy, reaching over 20,000 students.

Introduction

This book is a comprehensive guide for leaders who are at the forefront of the challenge of creating or managing effective software teams. It offers practical wisdom for building and leading high-performing teams.

This book delves into key areas pivotal for any software leader:

- **Building a high-performance team:** Discover the art and science of crafting a technology team that exceeds conventional performance metrics. This section delves into effective team assembly techniques and strategies to build high-impact teams.

- **Project Management:** Master the complexities of project management in the tech sector. This chapter equips you with the skills to manage the critical balance of time, scope, and budget using agile methodologies, risk mitigation strategies, and leadership techniques that ensure your team remains on course and efficient.

- **Code Quality:** Dive into the fundamentals of writing high-quality code that is maintainable, scalable, and efficient. Learn about essential practices, tools, and standards that contribute to the development of robust software products.

- **Software Design and Architecture:** Gain a deeper understanding of the principles underpinning effective software design and architecture. Explore how to build systems that not only fulfill current requirements but are also flexible enough to adapt to future challenges and expansion.

- **Software Development Life Cycle (SDLC):** Examine each phase of the SDLC, from inception to deployment. This section offers practical advice on enhancing processes to achieve smooth progress and high-quality results at every stage.

- **Software Quality Assurance:** Understand the pivotal role of quality assurance in the software development cycle. Learn the best practices for testing, continuous integration, and deployment that maintain the integrity and reliability of your software.

- **Observability:** Unravel the concept of observability and its significance in managing and troubleshooting software systems. This chapter discusses how to implement effective monitoring, logging, and analytical practices that enable deep insights and proactive problem resolution.

- **Technology and Business Alignment:** Explore the dynamic between technology and business objectives. This part guides you on aligning IT strategies with business goals to drive growth, improve customer satisfaction, and enhance competitive advantage.

Each chapter is not just a set of theories; rather, it's a collection of actionable insights and unconventional strategies that you can implement immediately.

Whether you're forming a new team, scaling an existing one, or striving to enhance your team's efficiency and creativity, the insights in this book will serve as your playbook. You'll find practical advice tailored to real-world challenges, backed by examples from my own journey in the tech world.

This book is designed for leaders who aspire to do more than just manage—to truly deliver value and uplift their teams. It's for those who believe in the power of good software practices and are ready to embrace the responsibilities and rewards of tech leadership.

Join me on this journey to explore the intricacies of leading successful software teams, where each chapter brings you closer to mastering the art of tech leadership.

Preface

With over 14 years of experience in both small startups and large corporations, I've observed a significant gap in professional leadership within the tech industry. Despite the pivotal role leadership plays in a team's success, I've rarely encountered companies that employ **structured, best-practice-driven leadership methods**. This widespread oversight often leads to recurrent issues that, although well-known within the industry, persist due to a lack of adherence to established standards and principles.

This realization sparked my motivation to share the insights I've gathered while building and leading teams in various roles, including as a principal engineer, team lead, and engineering manager. My journey has proven that applying specific principles and best practices can markedly improve team performance across different settings.

Tech Leadership Playbook is designed to be an indispensable resource for leaders tasked with the challenge of building or managing effective software development teams. This book is based on practical wisdom, offering actionable guidance to foster high-performing teams that excel in their projects.

By addressing common pitfalls through the adoption of proven best practices, and by cultivating a culture that emphasizes effective leadership practices, this book arms leaders with the crucial knowledge and tools needed to successfully navigate the complexities of contemporary business environments. I hope that by sharing these strategies, tech teams will be better positioned to sidestep frequent challenges and realize their full potential.

CHAPTER 1

Building High-Performance Teams

At the core of every successful organization lies a high-performance team, a group not just defined by its achievements but also by the synergy of its members. Building such a team is both an art and a science, requiring more than just assembling skilled individuals. It demands a holistic approach that intertwines good people, efficient processes, clear guidelines, effective communication, strategic automation, and a positive mindset.

In this chapter, we will explore the fundamental building blocks necessary for crafting a team that not only meets but exceeds expectations. The focus will be on the importance of recruiting good people—the bedrock of any team. We'll delve into the creation and implementation of good processes that streamline workflow and maximize efficiency. Equally crucial are good guidelines that provide direction and foster a culture of accountability.

A. Souza, *Tech Leadership Playbook*, https://doi.org/10.1007/979-8-8688-0543-1_1

Effective communication stands as a pillar of team dynamics, ensuring that ideas flow seamlessly and misunderstandings are minimized. Automation, when implemented wisely, can free up valuable time for creative and strategic tasks, pushing the team's productivity to new heights. Above all, the right mindset—one that embraces challenges, fosters growth, and values collaboration—can transform a group of individuals into a formidable team.

However, the performance of a team is not solely determined by these components. It is profoundly influenced by the culture and environment in which it operates. A supportive, inclusive, and empowering environment acts as a catalyst, propelling a team toward excellence. A positive culture nurtures each member's potential, fostering a spirit of unity and purpose.

In the pages that follow, we will dissect these elements, understanding how they interplay to create an environment where high-performance teams can thrive. This journey will reveal that building such a team is not just about the tangible metrics of success but also about cultivating an ethos where excellence is a natural outcome.

Hiring Good Engineers: The Keystone of Tech Leadership

This chapter dives into the critical task of not just filling positions, but finding the right people who can drive your team forward. As a tech lead, identifying and attracting top talent is your most pivotal role, and it involves a nuanced understanding of what truly makes an engineer valuable.

Central to this pursuit is the recognition that teams are made up of people, and the quality of these people determines the team's success. While technical skills are vital, they should be weighed equally with soft skills, and crucially, a sense of ownership. An engineer with ownership takes initiative, feels responsible for the success of the project, and consistently seeks ways to improve both the product and the process.

During the hiring process, your focus should be on uncovering a candidate's strengths, particularly their propensity for ownership and accountability. It's about finding individuals who bring a unique blend of skills and attitudes that complement and enhance the team dynamics. This means moving away from the traditional quest for "rockstar" individuals and, instead, building a team characterized by strength, cohesion, and collective ownership.

Seek out professionals who demonstrate a love for what they do and who have shown a pattern of learning and successfully applying new skills. Their engagement with the broader software development industry and open source communities can offer valuable insights into their commitment and growth potential.

When designing your hiring process, ensure it's inclusive and aimed at identifying true talent, not merely filtering out candidates based on their ability to recall information in an interview setting. Prioritize candidates' operational experience, problem-solving skills, and, importantly, their ability to foresee and address issues proactively.

Your team needs more than reactive problem solvers; it needs proactive thinkers. Engineers who can identify problems before they impact your customers, who can foresee growth areas, and who work proactively, are invaluable. These are the "innovation agents" and "efficiency improvers"—the individuals who don't just tackle the problems of today but anticipate and prepare for the challenges of tomorrow.

In conclusion, hiring is not about putting candidates through grueling tests to predict future performance. It's about identifying those with a growth mindset and nurturing them into roles where they can thrive, bringing a sense of ownership and forward-thinking to every challenge they encounter. Every successful founder talks about how at a certain point in the company's history, people become your best capital and your biggest asset.

Effective Interviewing: Real-World Questions for Software Developers

These interview questions are excellent for evaluating a candidate's real-world experience, problem-solving skills, and technical knowledge. They shift the focus from abstract puzzles to practical scenarios and concepts that are more relevant to everyday work in software development. Here's a brief analysis of each question, highlighting what they aim to assess:

- **Past Achievements**: "Tell me something that you have done in your previous job that you are proud of?"—This question assesses a candidate's achievements and what they value in their work. It can reveal their passion, initiative, and impact in previous roles.

- **Understanding Web development**: "Describe how a session is established between the browser (web app) and the backend app?"—Tests understanding of web technologies.

- **Language-Specific Knowledge**: "What is the default way your programming language stores session information?"—Assesses knowledge of language-specific features and best practices.

- **Transaction Integrity**: "In a money transfer between two accounts, how to guarantee that the money has been debited from account A and added to account B and how to avoid inconsistency in case of error when crediting to account B?"—Evaluates understanding of transactional integrity, database operations, and possibly Atomicity, Consistency, Isolation, and Durability (ACID) properties.

- **Programming Principles**: "Which is your favorite programming principle?"—Reveals the candidate's approach to coding and what principles guide their software development process.

- **Use of Design Patterns**: "What are the design patterns that you often see in place?"—Assesses familiarity with and practical application of design patterns in software development.

- **Identifying Bottlenecks**: "What are usually the bottlenecks of an application?"—Tests understanding of performance issues, scalability, and system optimization.

- **Database Performance Troubleshooting**: "If you have a performance issue in the database, one query is too slow, what would be your steps to try to identify and solve the problem?"—Evaluates problem-solving skills and knowledge of database performance tuning.

- **Distributed Systems Knowledge**: "How is your knowledge about distributed systems? Would you be able to point out the main challenges?"—Assesses understanding of distributed computing, its challenges, and complexities.

- **Scalability Considerations**: "What makes an application hard to be scalable?"—Tests understanding of scalability principles and the challenges in scaling applications.

- **Distributed Transactions**: "Bank account transfer example in a distributed system. How to guarantee that the money has been debited from account A and added to account B where each account is in a distinct system?"—A deeper dive into distributed transactions.

- **Continuous Deployment Implementation**: "Can you describe an implementation of continuous deployment?"—Assesses knowledge of DevOps practices, CI/CD pipelines, and automation.

- **Architecture Design**: "How would you architect a real-time dashboard?"—Tests architectural design skills, understanding of real-time data processing, and possibly front-end development.

- **Keeping Up with Technology**: "Talk about the (Your programing language)ecosystem and releases, how often is a new version released?"—Evaluates how well the candidate stays updated with their technology stack and its ecosystem.

These questions collectively provide a comprehensive view of a candidate's technical abilities, problem-solving skills, and adaptability to real-world scenarios in software development. They are effective in identifying candidates who are not only technically proficient but also capable of applying their knowledge practically and creatively.

Developing a Career Progression Plan

In today's competitive landscape, finding and keeping talented engineers is a significant challenge. Attracting and retaining such valuable talent is crucial. In a field driven by opportunities for growth and advancement, providing a well-defined career path is vital. It's not just about ensuring individual fulfillment; a structured career trajectory is also fundamental to maintaining organizational stability and fostering growth.

This section delves into the importance of establishing a clear career ladder that offers an environment for professional development.

Creating an effective career progression involves coordination across multiple departments. This collaboration ensures that the career progression framework is holistic, catering to the diverse needs and expectations within a tech company. It's crucial to recognize that there is no one-size-fits-all approach to career development. Different organizations, and indeed different roles within the same organization, may require unique career progression structures.

Utilizing Radar Charts to Help Develop Career Progression and Competencies

A practical tip for organizations looking to develop their career ladder is the use of radar charts. Radar charts can be an effective tool to visually represent the different competencies and expectations associated with each position within the company (Figure 1-1). By graphically displaying these dimensions, radar charts can help clarify the skills and achievements necessary at each career level.

The use of radar charts as a practical tool serves a dual purpose. Firstly, it provides a clear visual representation of the skills and competencies expected at various career levels. Secondly, it helps in setting transparent and achievable goals for professional development, allowing engineers to understand and work toward the requirements of their desired career trajectory, and engineering managers to have meaningful conversations with their direct reports around the expectations of each position and how to plan for the next level in their career ladder.

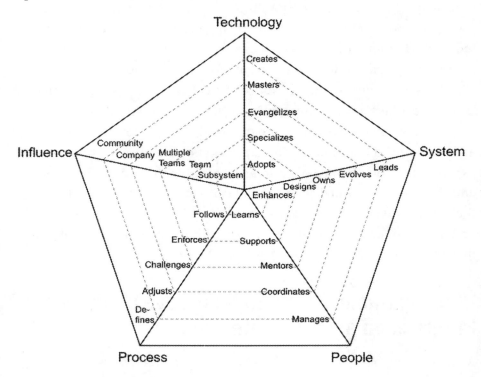

Figure 1-1. *Radar chart*

As a tangible example, I will provide radar charts for three key engineering roles: Entry-level Engineer (Figure 1-2), Senior Engineer (Figure 1-3), and Tech Lead Engineer (Figure 1-4), followed by a brief description of each. These charts will serve as a visual guide to the competencies and expectations associated with each of these levels, offering a clear and concise reference for both employees seeking career advancement and leaders tasked with guiding their development.

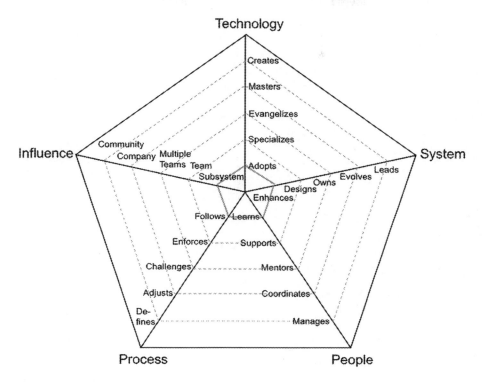

Figure 1-2. *Entry-level Radar chart*

Entry-level engineer characteristics:

- **Adopts**: actively learns and adopts the technology and tools defined by the team

- **Enhances**: successfully pushes new features and bug fixes to improve and extend the system

- **Learns**: quickly learns from others and consistently steps up when it is required

- **Follows**: follows the team processes, delivering a consistent flow of features to production

- **Subsystem**: makes an impact on one or more subsystems or team pods

9

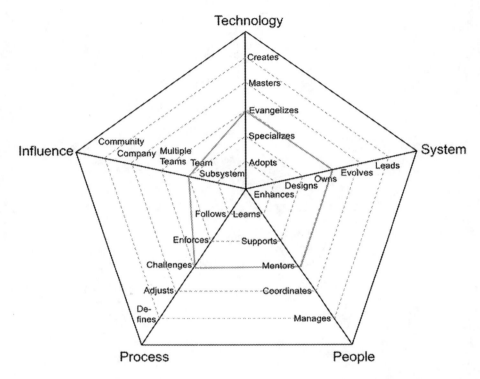

Figure 1-3. *Senior engineer Radar chart*

Senior engineer characteristics:

- **Evangelizes**: Researches, creates proofs of concept, and introduces new technologies to the team

- **Owns**: Owns the production operation and monitoring of the system and is aware of its SLAs

- **Mentors**: Mentors others to accelerate their career-growth and encourages them to participate

- **Challenges**: Challenges the team processes, looking for ways to improve them

- **Team**: Makes an impact on the whole team, not just on specific parts of it

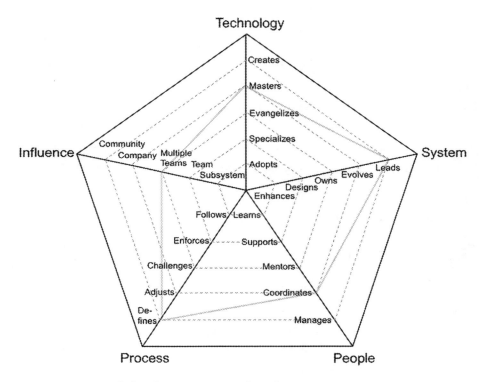

Figure 1-4. *Tech lead engineer Radar chart*

Tech lead engineer characteristics:

- **Masters**: Has very deep knowledge about the whole technology stack of the system

- **Leads**: Leads the technical excellence of the system and creates plans to mitigate outages

- **Coordinates**: Coordinates team members providing effective feedback and moderating discussions

- **Defines**: Defines the right processes for the team's maturity level, balancing agility, and discipline

- **Multiple Teams**: Makes an impact not only on the whole team but also on other teams

In summary, the establishment of a well-thought-out career ladder is imperative in the tech industry. It fosters a culture of continuous learning and growth, ensuring that both the individuals and the organization can thrive in an ever-evolving technological landscape. As the industry continues to grow and change, so too will the approaches to career development, requiring ongoing adaptation and refinement of these frameworks.

Crafting an Effective Full-Stack Team Structure

This section focuses on the ideal composition of a full-stack team, a structure that not only fosters efficiency and innovation but also ensures end-to-end (e2e) ownership of the product.

A full-stack team is more than just a group of individuals who can handle both front-end and back-end development. It's a holistic unit that embodies a range of skills, experiences, and perspectives. By embracing this diversity in skills and levels, the team creates an environment ripe for growth and mentorship. Senior members provide guidance and share their wealth of knowledge, while junior members bring fresh ideas and new approaches, creating a dynamic learning culture.

The key to a successful full-stack team lies in its independence and self-sufficiency. A team that has end-to-end ownership of a product is empowered to make decisions, respond to challenges, and innovate without being hindered by external dependencies. This autonomy accelerates the development process and enhances the team's sense of responsibility and commitment to the product.

Incorporating testers and operations personnel directly into the team is another critical aspect of this structure. While they may not need to be full-time members, their integration ensures that testing and operational considerations are not afterthoughts but integral parts of the development life cycle. This approach eliminates the need for external dependencies on other functional teams, streamlining the development process and fostering a more collaborative environment.

The Pitfalls of Functional Teams and the Power of Multi-skilled Unity

In this section, we will talk about the importance of building multi-skilled teams and steering clear of the pitfalls associated with functional, siloed teams.

A fundamental principle in modern software development is the embracement of teams that encompass a range of skills and responsibilities. These teams handle the entire application life cycle—from development, through deployment, to ongoing maintenance and updates. This end-to-end responsibility ensures that the team is not just accountable for each step of the process but also deeply invested in the success of the product. It eliminates dependencies on other teams during the release cycle, thereby streamlining processes and reducing time-to-market.

In the realm of software development, certain terms have often been misunderstood or misapplied. For instance, "DevOps" is not just a team; it's a culture and a set of practices that foster collaboration between development and operations teams. Similarly, the concept of a separate "Test team" is becoming obsolete. Quality assurance should be an integral part of the development process, with the entire team responsible for the quality of the product.

The problem with siloed functional teams—such as distinct Development, Operations, or Testing teams—is that it often leads to bottlenecks, miscommunications, and a fragmented understanding of the project. This separation can slow down processes, create a lack of ownership, and result in challenges in aligning toward a common goal.

In summary, the move away from functional teams toward an integrated, multi-skilled team approach is not just a trend, but a necessary evolution in the world of software development. It encourages a more agile, responsive, and collaborative environment, one that is better suited to meet the demands of modern software projects and deliver exceptional results.

Empowering Teams Through Ownership and Autonomy

The concept of team ownership and autonomy has emerged as a pivotal factor in driving innovation, efficiency, and employee satisfaction. Teams with end-to-end accountability are not only more motivated but also more equipped to creatively address high-value problems. This empowerment comes from seeing the direct impact of their work and understanding their role in the larger organizational picture.

The focus of this section is on the profound effect that ownership and autonomy have on the daily work of developers. When teams are given the freedom to make decisions and manage their tasks without excessive dependencies or delays, they achieve a state of "Flow." This state, characterized by deep focus and engagement in their work, leads not only to higher productivity but also to a sense of joy and fulfillment in their roles.

As Dan Pink says in his book:

We have three innate psychological needs — competence, autonomy, and relatedness. When those needs are satisfied, we're motivated, productive, and happy.

—Dan Pink

Building mission-oriented (Figure 1-5) teams further enhances this approach. By structuring teams around specific missions or goals, rather than individual tasks or functions, we create an environment where everyone is aligned toward a common objective. This alignment fosters collaboration, enhances focus, and ensures that all team members are working toward the same end result, driving the overall success of the project.

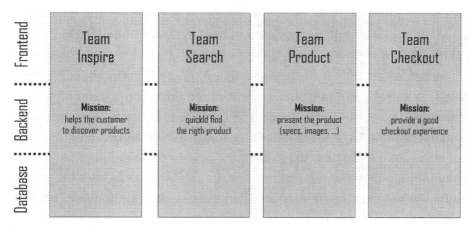

Figure 1-5. *Mission-oriented teams*

Cultivating Psychological Safety and a Blameless Culture

In the realm of team dynamics and productivity, the concept of psychological safety stands as a cornerstone for effective teamwork and innovation. Fostering an environment where team members feel safe to discuss challenges, admit mistakes, and share ideas without fear of retribution or ridicule. Creating a safety net for the team is not just about nurturing comfort; it's about unlocking the team's potential to tackle problems honestly and innovatively.

The perspective of viewing failures as opportunities for improvement is fundamental in this approach. Recognizing that most people come to work with the intention of doing well, it becomes evident that mistakes are not a result of a lack of effort or competence, but often a byproduct of complex systems and processes. By shifting the focus from blame to understanding, teams can uncover systemic issues and work collectively toward more robust solutions.

As demonstrated by the findings of <u>Google's Project Aristotle</u>, a culture that embraces risk-taking, admits faults, and learns from them is crucial for a team's effectiveness. Such a culture is built on the premise that psychological safety is the bedrock for candid conversations and innovative problem-solving. When team members feel secure in expressing their thoughts and concerns, it fosters a collaborative environment where prevention and continuous improvement are prioritized.

The core message of this section is clear: when team members are assured that they can speak openly about problems, mistakes, and new ideas without fear of blame or ridicule, they are more likely to engage in constructive problem-solving and innovation. This approach transforms failures and setbacks into powerful learning opportunities, enhancing the team's ability to adapt and improve.

Enhancing Team Collaboration for Optimal Performance

Team collaboration forms the bedrock of success in dynamic and complex fields like software development. It transcends mere cooperation, representing a synergy of efforts aimed at a common goal. This section explores the pivotal role of leadership in fostering a culture of collaboration and offers practical strategies to bolster team interaction and effectiveness.

Leadership is fundamentally responsible for creating an environment where collaboration thrives. This involves cultivating open communication, mutual respect, and shared responsibility. A collaborative environment is one where team members are not only involved in the project life cycle but are also encouraged to engage in open dialogue, share feedback, and ask questions without hesitation.

To enhance team collaboration, consider these strategies:

- **Open Communication**: Encourage team members to freely give feedback and ask questions, fostering a culture of openness and trust.

- **Code Ownership**: Move away from the concept of selective ownership of code. Embrace a shared responsibility approach to improve collective code quality and learning.

- **Knowledge Sharing**: Implement regular sessions for knowledge exchange within the team, ensuring everyone benefits from shared expertise.

- **Fair Task Distribution**: Allocate tasks equitably, allowing all team members to grow and contribute meaningfully.

- **Synchronous Interaction**: Facilitate real-time interactions like chats, calls, screen sharing, and in-person meetings for clearer and immediate communication.

- **Rapid Response**: Cultivate a culture where responding swiftly to unblock team members is prioritized.

- **Disagree and Commit Principle**: Encourage a mindset where the team's success and delivery are prioritized over individual preferences.

- **Decision Record and Best Practices:** Use decision records, principles, and best practices to streamline decision-making processes and avoid unnecessary discussions.

- **Team Fun Activities**: Promote team-building and fun activities. Regular informal gatherings, virtual games, or team outings can strengthen relationships and improve team cohesion.

As we conclude this exploration into fostering team collaboration, it is clear that the strength of a team lies not just in the individual skills of its members, but in how effectively they work together toward a common goal. The strategies discussed in this section are essential tools for building a cohesive, dynamic, and productive team environment.

The Power of Team Principles Document in Software Development

In the dynamic world of software development, the success of a team hinges not just on skills and processes, but also on the underlying principles guiding the team's actions and decisions.

This chapter delves into how Team principles document can enhance the effectiveness of the team and help to influence team members toward common engineering principles and a culture of effectiveness and quality. It acts as a common language, aligning every team member's thinking toward shared goals and strategies.

This guiding helps in decision-making and discussions, providing clarity that transcends specific situations or temporary individual emotions.

Furthermore, team principles set clear expectations for both existing and new members. They can be an integral part of the hiring process, giving potential recruits a glimpse into the team's working style and values.

Principles cover generalities, allow adaptation to unforeseen circumstances, don't put people in a box, and enable team members to use their best judgment and be innovative.

While it's often recommended that team principles be created collaboratively, I propose a slightly different approach. Initially, these principles should be crafted by the tech leadership, providing a foundational ethos for the team. As the team matures, these principles can be revisited and refined collaboratively, ensuring they remain relevant and resonant with the team's evolving dynamics.

Here are ten examples of principles to consider:

- Divide tasks fairly and square, making sure the whole team is growing.

- It is essential that the team give feedback and ask questions.

- Fast response within the team—Unblocking the team member is the priority.

- Ensure psychological safety and blamelessness. We see failures as an opportunity to improve systems and processes.

- Choose to work on improving productivity over working on a feature.

- Make sure self-initiatives get the due recognition.

- Regularly reflect on how to become more effective.

- Measure progress and productivity by the amount of value delivered.

- Continuous improvement is better than delayed perfection.

- Be proud of our work.

- Choose simplicity over clever or complex solutions(KISS).

- YAGNI—you aren't going to need it.

- Follow <u>Agile principles</u>.

Remember, the creation of team principles, initially led by tech leadership, is not a one-time event but a continuous journey. As the team matures, involving them in the evolution of these principles can lead to greater buy-in and a deeper understanding of what makes your team unique and successful.

In closing, the adoption of well-crafted team principles document is a powerful step toward building a culture of excellence in software development. These principles are the compass that guides your team, ensuring that each member not only excels in their individual roles but also contributes to the greater success of the team. As you move forward, let these principles be your guide, your inspiration, and your benchmark for success.

Building Team Alignment for Effective Decision-Making

In team environments, the approach to decision-making can significantly impact the dynamics and outcomes of group collaboration. Contrary to the popular belief that democratic voting is the most effective way to reach consensus, this method can sometimes undermine true teamwork and collaboration. This section will explore more nuanced and inclusive strategies for decision-making that focus on team alignment rather than majority rule.

The shortcomings of democratic voting in team settings are multifaceted:

- **Focus on Winning Arguments**: The process often shifts toward winning a debate for votes, overshadowing the collaborative spirit of working as a unified team.

- **Dominance of Majority**: This approach can enable a majority to impose their views, potentially marginalizing minority opinions and causing disengagement.

- **Stifling New Ideas**: Quick voting on new proposals can lead to premature dismissal of innovative ideas, particularly if they are not immediately popular or well-understood.

The initial step in any decision-making process is to ensure the decision aligns with the team's principles. This alignment is crucial as it ensures that any decision is in harmony with the team's core values and objectives.

After establishing this alignment, the next vital step is building team alignment. Rather than simply achieving consensus, building alignment involves gaining a collective understanding and commitment to a decision. Here, the role of a team leader is pivotal. The leader should mediate the conversation, ensuring that discussions remain focused on the topic and do not become personal. It is also the leader's responsibility to ensure that everyone understands the pros and cons of each decision, fostering an informed and balanced dialogue.

The Fist to Five technique (Figure 1-6) is a practical tool in this process. It allows team members to visually express their level of agreement with a decision, providing a quick and inclusive way to gauge opinions. It also provides a clear indication of the team's stance and helping identify areas that might need further discussion.

Fist to Five technique works as follows:

- **Fist**: Indicates strong disagreement or a veto.

- **One or Two Fingers**: Signifies major reservations.

- **Three Fingers**: Shows some agreement but with reservations or questions.

- **Four Fingers**: Means agreement, but not total.

- **Five Fingers**: Signifies full agreement.

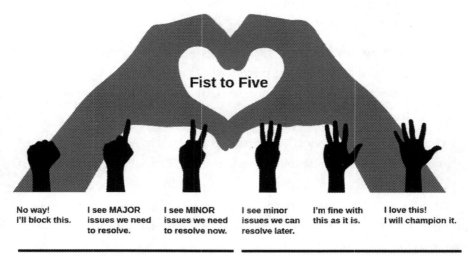

Figure 1-6. *Fist to five*

This section has highlighted the importance of moving from a mindset of "winning a vote" to "building alignment." By doing so, teams can leverage the collective intelligence and perspectives of all members, leading to decisions that are robust, well-considered, and broadly supported.

In conclusion, the journey toward effective team decision-making is one of continuous learning and adaptation. It involves embracing techniques that foster alignment and understanding the pivotal role of leadership in guiding these processes. As teams adopt these practices, they become more cohesive, agile, and capable of tackling complex challenges with confidence and unity.

Navigating the Five Stages of Team Development

Building a successful team is a dynamic and evolving process, and it's unrealistic to expect a new team to excel from the outset. Understanding the stages a team goes through on its path to high performance is crucial for any leader or team member.

The Psychologist Bruce Tuckman has created a model that describes the path that most teams follow on their way to high performance. He identified four stages: Forming, Storming, Norming, and Performing (Figure 1-7).

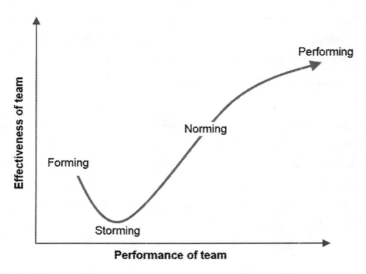

Figure 1-7. *Team phases*

- **Forming**: In this initial stage, team members come together, often with a mix of excitement and anxiety. They orient themselves to the task at hand and start forming relationships within the group. This phase is generally positive and polite, but it's more about individual orientation than team cohesion.

- **Storming**: Often the most tumultuous stage, Storming is marked by the establishment of team roles, which can lead to conflicts and power struggles. It's a critical phase where the team's future can hang in the balance. Navigating this stage requires careful management of interpersonal dynamics and conflicts.

- **Norming:** As the team moves into the Norming stage, a consensus begins to form. Members develop trust, actively engage in the project, and show respect for each other's opinions. The team starts to feel more cohesive and motivated toward the common goal.

- **Performing**: In this final stage identified by Tuckman, the team reaches its full potential. Members are collaborative, supportive, and flexible in their roles. The focus is on collective success rather than individual achievements.

Recognizing the characteristics and challenges of each phase allows leaders and team members to navigate the journey more effectively and with greater empathy.

- **Forming**: Emphasizes the importance of setting clear goals and expectations while fostering positive relationships.

- **Storming**: Highlights the need for strong leadership to navigate conflicts and clarify roles, ensuring the team stays cohesive.

- **Norming**: Shows the value of building trust and collaboration, setting the stage for effective teamwork.

- **Performing**: Demonstrates the power of a cohesive team working in unison toward a common goal, with flexibility in roles and a focus on collective success.

The journey through these stages is not always linear. Teams may cycle back through stages as they face new challenges or changes in their environment. However, understanding these stages equips teams with the knowledge to handle these dynamics constructively.

Conclusion

Building a high-performance team is an ongoing process that demands commitment, awareness, and continuous improvement. Such teams are the engines of innovation and success in any organization, capable of achieving exceptional results and driving sustainable growth. As leaders and team members, the pursuit of excellence in team performance is a journey that is challenging yet immensely rewarding.

Key Takeaways

1. **Hiring and Cultivating Talent**: At the core of high-performance teams are skilled and motivated engineers. Emphasizing not only technical abilities but also soft skills and a strong sense of ownership ensures that team members are not only competent but also deeply invested in the project's success.

2. **Enhancing Interviewing Techniques**: By moving away from abstract theoretical questions to those that reflect real-world challenges, we ensure that the hiring process is aligned with the practical needs of software development, thereby securing talent that is ready to contribute effectively from day one.

3. **Career Development**: Utilizing tools like radar charts to map out career progression helps clarify expectations and growth paths within the team, fostering a motivated and forward-looking workforce.

4. **Optimal Team Structures**: Shifting from functional teams to a full-stack, multi-skilled team structure enhances flexibility and responsiveness, allowing teams to manage a variety of challenges more efficiently.

5. **Ownership and Autonomy**: Empowering teams by delegating ownership and encouraging autonomous decision-making leads to higher motivation and productivity, as team members feel more connected to the outcomes of their work.

6. **Psychological Safety and a Blameless Culture**: Establishing a safe environment where team members feel secure to express ideas and concerns without fear of blame is essential for innovative and risk-taking behaviors, which are critical to technological advancement and problem-solving.

7. **Effective Collaboration and Communication**: Tools like the Fist to Five technique aid in building alignment and ensuring that every team member is on board with decisions, thereby enhancing team cohesion and the effectiveness of collaborative efforts.

8. **Adhering to Team Principles**: A well-documented set of team principles acts as a guiding beacon for all team members, aligning efforts and fostering a culture of quality and effectiveness.

9. **Understanding Team Dynamics**: Navigating through the Five Stages of Team Development with awareness and proactive management ensures that teams mature into highly effective units capable of tackling complex software projects.

CHAPTER 2

Agile Project Management

In the ever-evolving landscape of software development, agility is not merely an advantage but a necessity. This chapter delves into the dynamic world of Agile project management, a methodology that has transformed the way teams develop software, respond to changes, and deliver value to stakeholders. Through a focus on Agile principles, we aim to provide a comprehensive guide to mastering effective project management techniques that are crucial in today's fast-paced tech environment.

Agile project management is more than just a set of practices; it is a mindset that emphasizes flexibility, continuous improvement, and a high level of involvement from team members and stakeholders alike. At the heart of this approach are Agile estimation and planning—techniques that ensure projects remain adaptable and measurable without sacrificing the quality or scope of the work. We will explore methods to enhance these practices, ensuring they can be effectively applied regardless of project size or complexity.

Communication is the backbone of any successful project. This chapter will discuss strategies to improve interactions within teams and with stakeholders, ensuring that every voice is heard and that the project's vision and progress are clearly understood by all involved. Furthermore, we will examine how to structure work using Epics, User Stories, and Tasks to break down complex projects into manageable, actionable items that align with business goals and user needs.

Effective project management is also about the governance of processes and decisions. We'll outline guidelines for managing project decisions, maintaining detailed records, and conducting meetings that are not just obligatory gatherings but pivotal opportunities for course correction, brainstorming, and decisive action.

Additionally, the chapter will navigate through the nuances of different Agile frameworks such as Scrum and Kanban. Each framework offers unique benefits and can be tailored to suit specific project requirements. Understanding these can help teams choose the most appropriate one for their context.

Managing backlogs and tickets efficiently is critical to maintaining project momentum and clarity. We will cover proven strategies to manage backlogs effectively and to design ticket workflows that enhance clarity, priority setting, and accountability.

By the end of this chapter, you will be equipped with a solid foundation in Agile project management practices, ready to implement these strategies to lead projects that excel in delivering value efficiently and consistently.

Agile Software Project Management in a Nutshell

I will attempt to summarize project management in simple terms here, but I believe it would be more effective if you could watch an animated video that excellently outlines Agile Software Product Management in a nutshell (Figure 2-1). Watching the video is crucial because I want it to inspire you with its depiction of a flexible and iterative approach to managing Software projects. The video can be viewed here: https://youtu.be/5o2ILHjX9EE?

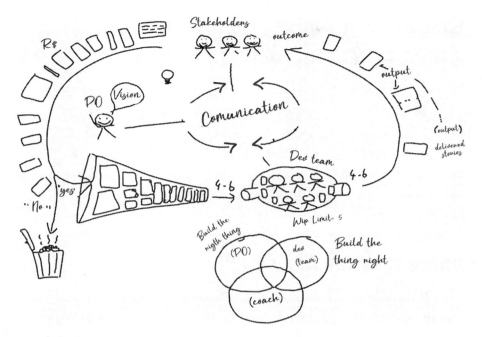

Figure 2-1. *Agile project management in a nutshell*

Agile Software Project Management is a powerful and adaptive tool that offers a stark departure from traditional waterfall methodologies. It is an iterative approach to software delivery that builds software incrementally from the start of the project, instead of trying to deliver it all at once near the end. It works by breaking projects down into little bits of user functionality called user stories, prioritizing them, and then continuously delivering them in short cycles called iterations. Whether a team is new to Agile or looking to improve their processes, embracing Agile principles is a step toward building software that better meets user needs and adapts swiftly to the ever-changing demands of the digital world.

Embracing the Agile Manifesto in Modern Software Development

Introduced in 2001 by a group of forward-thinking developers, The Agile Manifesto was a response to the limitations of traditional, rigid software development methodologies. It emphasizes flexibility, collaboration, customer satisfaction, and the delivery of high-value products. This section delves into the Agile Manifesto, highlighting its enduring relevance and the principles that have become fundamental in managing modern software projects.

Summary of the Agile Manifesto

The Agile Manifesto, formulated in 2001 by a group of experienced software developers, marked a significant shift in the approach to software development. It was born out of a need to find an alternative to the traditional, rigid, and linear methodologies that dominated the industry. The manifesto is centred around four core values and twelve guiding principles that emphasize adaptability, collaboration, customer focus, and efficiency.

Core Values

- **Individuals and Interactions Over Processes and Tools**: Prioritizing direct communication and collaboration over rigid adherence to tools and processes.

- **Working Software Over Comprehensive Documentation**: Focusing on delivering functional and valuable software over exhaustive documentation.

- **Customer Collaboration Over Contract Negotiation**: Encouraging continuous customer involvement and feedback instead of relying solely on contractual obligations.

- **Responding to Change Over Following a Plan**: Embracing change and being flexible in planning to address evolving project needs effectively.

Guiding Principles

The twelve principles further elaborate on these values, emphasizing aspects like customer satisfaction through early and continuous delivery, welcoming changing requirements, delivering working software frequently, close collaboration between business stakeholders and developers, motivated individuals, face-to-face conversation, sustainable development pace, technical excellence, simplicity, self-organizing teams, and regular reflection on how to become more effective.

The Agile Manifesto represents a paradigm shift from the traditional waterfall model, advocating for a more iterative, flexible, and collaborative approach to software development. It's not just a methodology but a mindset that values human communication and feedback, adapts to change, and focuses on delivering tangible results.

Relevance of Agile Values and Principles

Despite the evolution in technology and project management tools, the values and principles laid out in the Agile Manifesto remain as relevant today as they were two decades ago. They continue to drive the way software projects are managed, focusing on iterative development, early and continuous delivery of value, and frequent feedback loops. These principles have proven effective in ensuring that software development is adaptive, customer-focused, and geared toward delivering functional, high-quality products in a timely manner.

Iterative Development and Continuous Delivery

A key highlight of Agile is its iterative nature and the emphasis on constant and early value delivery. Agile teams work in cycles, allowing for regular reassessment of project priorities and adjustments to plans. This iterative approach ensures that the product evolves with the changing needs of the customer and the market.

Frequent Feedback Loops

Agile also fosters a culture of frequent feedback (Figure 2-2), both from customers and within the team. This ongoing feedback loop is integral in ensuring that the product aligns with customer needs and expectations, and it allows teams to rapidly respond to changes and challenges.

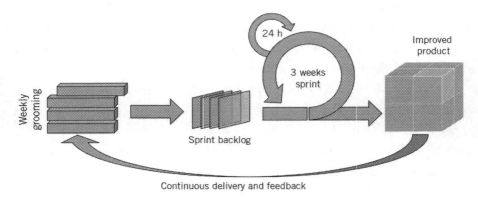

Figure 2-2. *Frequent feedbak loop*

In conclusion, while The Agile Manifesto provides the philosophical framework for Agile development, it doesn't delve into the specifics of practical processes and techniques. The manifesto sets the stage, but it's the various Agile methodologies and practices that bring the performance to life.

In the following sections, we will explore some of these practical Agile processes and techniques. We'll dive into specific practices, examine tools that facilitate Agile project management, and discuss techniques for effective implementation in real-world scenarios.

For those interested in exploring the Agile Manifesto further, `https://agilemanifesto.org` is a link to the Agile Manifesto, providing deeper insights into its values and principles.

Understanding Scrum vs. Kanban in Agile Methodologies

In the realm of Agile methodologies, Scrum and Kanban stand out as two of the most widely adopted frameworks. While both are underpinned by Agile principles, they differ significantly in their approach, structure, and application. In this section, we will look at the differences and provide insights into when to use each methodology, helping teams and organizations choose the framework that best suits their needs.

Differences Between Scrum and Kanban

- **Framework Structure**: Scrum is structured around fixed-length iterations called sprints, typically lasting two to four weeks, where a set amount of work is completed. Kanban, on the other hand, is more fluid, focusing on continuous delivery without prescribed iteration lengths.

- **Roles and Ceremonies**: Scrum defines specific roles (Scrum Master, Product Owner, Development Team) and ceremonies (Sprint Planning, Daily Stand-up, Sprint Review, Sprint Retrospective). Kanban is less prescriptive, with no predefined roles or mandatory meetings.

- **Work Visualization and Limits**: Both methodologies use boards to visualize work, but Kanban emphasizes limiting work-in-progress (WIP) through its columns, whereas Scrum focuses on what can be achieved within a sprint.

- **Change Adaptability**: While Scrum encourages adaptability within sprints, Kanban offers more flexibility to change priorities and tasks on the fly.

- **Performance Metrics**: Scrum uses velocity as a key metric, measuring the amount of work completed in a sprint. Kanban focuses on cycle time, the time it takes to complete a single item.

When to Use Each Methodology

Choosing between Scrum and Kanban often depends on the team's context, project nature, and specific goals:

- **Use Scrum when**

  - You have a well-defined project with changes that are not expected to be frequent or drastic.

  - Your team benefits from the structure and discipline of sprints, roles, and ceremonies.

  - There is a need for regular, fixed deliverables or iterations.

- **Use Kanban when**

  - The project requires flexibility with frequent priority shifts and varying types of work items.

- Your team aims for a continuous flow of delivery without the constraints of timed iterations.

- You are looking to improve or optimize existing processes with a focus on workflow efficiency.

To bring these concepts to life, let's consider practical scenarios where Scrum and Kanban would be the most effective:

- **Scrum for New Projects**: Imagine you're kicking off a new software development project. The goals are clear, but the path to achieving them might require rigorous planning, regular reviews, and adjustments. In this scenario, Scrum is ideal. Its structured sprints allow the team to focus on delivering specific features or components within a set time frame, ensuring regular progress checks and the flexibility to pivot as needed based on sprint reviews. The defined roles and ceremonies in Scrum also help in establishing a clear operational framework for a new team still finding its rhythm.

- **Kanban for Maintaining Existing Projects**: Now, consider a team responsible for maintaining an existing software product. The work mainly involves managing a steady stream of bug tickets and incremental improvements. Here, Kanban is more suitable due to its flexibility and focus on managing ongoing tasks with varying priorities. Kanban's continuous flow model allows the team to quickly address bugs and update tasks without waiting for a new sprint, optimizing the team's response time and efficiency in handling maintenance work.

- **Transitioning to Scrumban**: As the new project matures and the team becomes more established, a transition to "Scrumban"—a hybrid of Scrum and Kanban—can be considered. This approach is beneficial in scenarios where the initial phase of the project has passed, and the team is moving toward a phase that requires managing a mix of new feature development and ongoing maintenance or bug fixes. Scrumban retains the structured elements of Scrum for new development work while incorporating the flexibility of Kanban for ongoing tasks. This hybrid approach allows teams to enjoy the benefits of both methodologies, adapting to the evolving needs of the project and the team.

By starting with Scrum and then transitioning to Scrumban, teams can effectively manage the life cycle of a project from its initiation through to its maturity, ensuring that the methodology evolves in tandem with the project's needs and the team's maturity.

Scrumban

Scrumban is an Agile methodology that merges the structured framework of Scrum with the flexibility and continuous improvement aspects of Kanban. It's designed to provide teams with a more adaptable approach to project management, particularly in environments where priorities shift frequently, and work demands are variable.

Key Features of Scrumban

- **Hybrid Structure**: Scrumban combines Scrum's iterative development and roles with Kanban's focus on workflow efficiency and limit on work-in-progress (WIP).

- **Flexible Planning**: Unlike Scrum's fixed-length sprints, Scrumban allows for continuous planning. Work items are pulled from the backlog as needed, offering a more fluid approach to task management.

- **Visual Workflow Management**: Utilizes a Kanban board to visualize task progress, enhancing transparency and communication within the team.

- **Adaptive Roles**: While incorporating roles from Scrum, Scrumban offers flexibility in roles and responsibilities, adapting to the needs of the team and project.

- **Continuous Improvement**: Emphasizes ongoing process improvement and efficiency, borrowing from Kanban's principle of regularly analyzing and optimizing the workflow.

- **Meeting Structure**: Retains key Scrum ceremonies like retrospectives and reviews but with a more flexible approach to scheduling and conducting these meetings.

- **Pull-Based System**: Tasks are "pulled" into the workflow based on team capacity and priority, ensuring a sustainable work pace and minimizing overload.

Benefits of Scrumban

- Ideal for projects with changing priorities or requirements.

- Enhances team flexibility and responsiveness to change.

- Balances structure with adaptability, offering a middle ground for teams transitioning from Scrum.

- Supports a sustainable pace of work without the rigidity of sprint deadlines.

- Encourages continuous improvement and efficiency in workflows.

Application of Scrumban

Scrumban is particularly effective in environments that require both the discipline of regular planning and the ability to adapt quickly to changing needs. It is well-suited for maintenance projects, evolving products, and environments where work demands fluctuate.

As we conclude our exploration of Scrum and Kanban, along with the transition to Scrumban, it's evident that each Agile methodology offers unique strengths and addresses different project management needs. The choice between Scrum and Kanban, and the decision to transition to Scrumban, should be guided by the specific demands and dynamics of your project and team.

In choosing the right methodology, consider factors like the nature of the project, team preferences, workflow complexity, and the level of change in project requirements. Remember, the ultimate goal of any Agile methodology is to enhance efficiency, adaptability, and team collaboration.

Ticket Management

Effective project management is deeply intertwined with efficient ticket management. Tickets, or work items, are the building blocks of any project, serving as a crucial tool for organizing, tracking, and executing tasks. Proper categorization and understanding of different ticket types not only bring clarity to the project's workflow but also significantly enhance team communication and productivity. This section will explore various types of tickets commonly used in project management and how they contribute to a project's success.

Different Types of Tickets:

- **Initiatives(Epics)**: Large-scale, high-level work items that encompass significant portions of a project. They usually span multiple sprints and are broad in scope. Example: "Add new payment provider."

- **Features**: These tickets represent new functionalities or enhancements from a user's perspective, complete with details and visual mockups. Initiated by the Product Owner, features are often described using the template: "As a (persona), I want to (do something) so that I can (achieve a goal)."

- **User Stories**: User Stories are more specific than features and focus directly on enhancing the end-user experience. They are also written from the user's perspective and can be created by either the Product Owner or the team.

- **SubTasks**: These are technical tasks linked to a user story, detailing the specific work that needs to be done to support the larger user story. Example: "Implement search product by name."

- **Tasks**: Tasks are technical work that may or may not be directly linked to a user story. They typically involve work that doesn't deliver direct value to the end user but is crucial for the project, such as addressing technical debt, infrastructure, or performance improvements.

- **Spikes**: Spikes are exploratory tasks aimed at gathering information or solving uncertainties that inform the refinement of a feature or user story. The output of a spike is a clearer and more defined user story or feature.

User-Facing vs. Technical Tickets

Distinguishing between user-facing tickets (like Features and User Stories) and technical tickets (like Tasks and Subtasks) is vital. User-facing tickets are directly related to the end-user experience and are typically more visible to stakeholders, while technical tickets often involve backend work that, although not immediately visible to users, is crucial for the system's functionality and stability. This differentiation helps in prioritizing tasks and allocating resources efficiently, ensuring that both user value and system integrity are maintained.

Communication and Value Delivery

The structured breakdown from Initiatives to Subtasks not only aids in project planning but also in communicating progress. It allows teams to clearly demonstrate how each task, no matter how technical or backend-focused, contributes to delivering value to the end user. This clarity is crucial for stakeholder engagement and aligning team efforts with user needs.

As we conclude this section on ticket management, it's clear that the way we categorize and handle tickets is more than just a task management exercise; it's a fundamental aspect of effective project management. By differentiating between user-facing and technical tickets and organizing work into defined groupings like Initiatives, Features, User Stories, and Subtasks, we gain a multilayered perspective of the project's progress, challenges, and achievements.

Key Takeaways

- **Clarity in Prioritization**: Distinguishing between different types of tickets—especially separating user-facing from technical tasks—plays a crucial role in prioritization and resource allocation. It ensures that while the end user needs drive the project's direction, the technical integrity of the product is not compromised.

- **Structured Approach to Task Management**: The hierarchy of Initiatives, Features, User Stories, and Subtasks creates a structured approach to managing tasks. This structure not only aids in detailed planning but also in tracking progress at different levels, from high-level visions to the minutiae of technical implementation.

- **Enhanced Communication**: This structured approach to ticket management enhances communication within the team and with stakeholders. It allows all parties to clearly understand how each piece of work, no matter how small or technical, contributes to the overarching goals and delivers value to the end user.

- **Adaptability and Continuous Improvement**: Effective ticket management is also about adaptability and continuous improvement. Regularly revisiting and reassessing ticket categories and their management can lead to more efficient processes and a better understanding of the project life cycle.

In summary, ticket management is a vital skill in Agile project management. It requires not only an understanding of the different types of work involved in a project but also an appreciation of how these different tasks interconnect to deliver a successful product.

Backlog Management for Streamlined Execution

Backlog management is a critical component of successful project execution in Agile methodologies. It involves more than just listing tasks; it's about strategically planning and organizing work items to ensure clear communication, effective tracking, and unwavering focus on agreed-upon goals. This section explores the nuances of backlog management, highlighting techniques such as the use of milestones and the "**Now**, **Next**, and **Later**" method to optimize the team's workflow and maintain momentum throughout the project life cycle.

Using Milestones Effectively

Milestones are pivotal checkpoints within a project that signify the completion of key phases or the achievement of significant objectives. Incorporating milestones into the backlog serves multiple purposes:

- **Provides a Sense of Progress**: Milestones offer tangible indicators of progress, giving the team and stakeholders a clear sense of how the project is advancing.

- **Fosters Accomplishment and Motivation**: Achieving milestones creates a sense of accomplishment, boosting team morale and motivation.

- **Guides Direction and Focus**: Setting milestones helps in aligning the team's efforts toward critical goals, ensuring that everyone remains focused on the most important tasks.

The "Now, Next, and Later" Technique

To further refine backlog management, the "Now, Next, and Later" technique can be employed. This approach involves categorizing tasks into three distinct time frames:

- **Now**: Tasks that are currently in progress or need immediate attention.

- **Next**: Tasks that are up next in the queue, ready to be tackled once the "Now" tasks are completed.

- **Later**: Longer-term tasks or those that don't require immediate action but are still important for the project's future stages.

This method not only simplifies prioritization but also provides a clear roadmap for the team, enabling them to understand what needs their attention immediately, what's coming up next, and what's planned for the future. This categorization aids in keeping the team focused and prepared, reducing overwhelm and increasing efficiency.

As we conclude this section on effective backlog management, it's evident that the way a team organizes and prioritizes its work items is crucial for the smooth execution and success of a project. Backlog management is not just a task listing exercise; it's a strategic process that requires careful planning, clear communication, and continuous adaptation.

Key Takeaways

- **Strategic Planning**: Organizing the backlog goes beyond mere task enumeration. It involves strategic planning to ensure that every work item aligns with the project's goals and delivers maximum value.

- **Milestones as Motivators**: The use of milestones in backlog management cannot be overstated. These checkpoints serve as tangible markers of progress, providing the team with a sense of accomplishment and direction. They help in maintaining focus on key deliverables and ensure that the project stays on track.

- **'Now, Next, and Later' Technique**: It offers a clear view of what the team needs to focus on immediately, what is upcoming, and what is planned for the future.

- **Communication and Clarity**: Effective backlog management enhances communication within the team and with stakeholders. It ensures that everyone involved has a clear understanding of the project's priorities, progress, and expectations.

In summary, mastering backlog management is key to the success of Agile projects. It requires a thoughtful approach to planning, a focus on key milestones, and a flexible mindset to adapt as the project evolves.

Effective Ticket Workflow in Agile Project Management

In Agile project management, the journey from the initial concept to the final implementation is both dynamic and structured. This section focuses on the team workflow, tracing the path from the creation of feature tickets to their planning and implementation. We will explore each stage of this process, providing insights into how teams can effectively manage and execute their tasks. This workflow is crucial for maintaining clarity, ensuring efficient progress, and achieving the project's goals in a systematic manner.

Creating and Categorizing Feature Tickets

- **Initial Creation**: The Product Owner (PO) initiates the process by creating a Feature ticket. This ticket encapsulates a significant functionality or enhancement for the product.

- **Labelling and Bucketing**: The PO labels the ticket as "user-stories/feature" and categorizes it under the appropriate bucket: NOW, NEXT, or LATER, based on its current priority and timeline.

Refining the Backlog

- **Prioritization**: During backlog refinement sessions, the team collaboratively reviews the NEXT bucket to determine which stories should be moved to NOW (prioritized for immediate action), left in NEXT, or moved to LATER (deprioritized).

- **Ready for Action**: User stories in the NOW bucket should either be fully refined and ready for implementation or linked with a spike (refinement ticket) for further clarification.

Breaking Down Features and User Stories

- **Feature Decomposition**: If a Feature is too large to be completed within a single sprint, the team breaks it down into smaller, more manageable User Stories.

- **User Story Decomposition**: For User Stories that span across multiple services or repositories, the team further breaks them down into specific tasks or subtasks to streamline implementation.

Implementing User Stories

- **Focused Implementation**: Once the implementation of a Feature or User Story begins, it should progress continuously to completion. The aim is to minimize Work-In-Progress (WIP) and avoid the fragmentation of focus across multiple ongoing Features or User Stories.

Planning Phases

- **Phase Planning**: When planning a new PHASE/ Milestone of the project, the team evaluates the LATER bucket to decide which issues should be included in the NEXT phase. Remember that the team are constantly looking at the NEXT bucket, as part of the periodic backlog refinement.

- **Roadmap Structuring**: The project roadmap is structured into several small, meaningful, and flexible phases/milestones. Examples of phases might include "Prototype Development," "Integration with Third-Party X," "Adding New Payment Provider," and "Implementation of Extra Features."

As we conclude this section on the Agile team workflow, from the creation of feature tickets to their planning and implementation, it's clear that a structured yet flexible approach is essential for the smooth progression of any software project. This workflow is not just a series of steps; it's a strategic framework that ensures efficiency, clarity, and focus throughout the project life cycle.

Key Takeaways

- **Structured Flexibility**: The workflow demonstrates the balance between structure and adaptability. While each stage has defined processes, there's room for adjustments based on the project's evolving needs.

- **Clarity and Prioritization**: The categorization of tickets into NOW, NEXT, and LATER buckets aids in clear prioritization and helps the team focus on immediate goals while keeping an eye on future tasks.

- **Collaborative Refinemen**t: Backlog refinement is a collaborative effort that ensures all team members are on the same page, leading to better understanding and efficient task execution.

- **Decomposition for Manageability**: Breaking down features and user stories into smaller, manageable tasks is crucial for maintaining a sustainable workload and ensuring that each element is given the attention it deserves.

- **Continuous Progress**: The emphasis on minimizing Work-In-Progress (WIP) and focusing on one task at a time leads to more concentrated effort and continuous progress.

- **Phase-based Planning**: Organizing the project into phases allows the team to achieve milestones systematically, providing a sense of accomplishment and clear direction.

- **Roadmap Flexibility**: The flexible nature of the roadmap allows for adaptability and change, which is essential in the Agile environment where requirements and priorities can shift.

In conclusion, the Agile team workflow provides a clear guide for teams to navigate the complexities of software development, ensuring that tasks are well-defined, prioritized, and executed efficiently.

Agile Estimation and Planning

In the Agile framework, the practice of estimation and planning holds a unique place. It's a process often met with skepticism, given the inherent uncertainties in software development. Yet, understanding why and how to estimate effectively is crucial for Agile teams. This section delves into the reasons behind Agile estimation, the pitfalls of traditional estimation methods, and the emphasis on value delivery as the ultimate metric of success.

Why Estimate?

In Agile project management, estimation often receives mixed reactions. Many practitioners question the value of estimates, especially when they rarely hit the mark exactly as predicted. "If our estimates are mostly wrong, why bother estimating at all?" is a common sentiment. However, the true purpose of estimation in Agile goes beyond merely predicting outcomes. **Estimation is fundamentally about communication, understanding, and effective planning**.

Why Estimation Matters in Agile

- **Gaining Shared Understanding of User Stories**

  Estimation is not just about attaching numbers to tasks; it's a process that facilitates deeper team discussions about user stories. Through the act of estimating, team members exchange ideas on the scope and complexity of tasks, which helps everyone involved gain a clearer and shared understanding of what needs to be done. This mutual understanding is crucial for aligning team efforts and ensuring everyone is on the same page.

- **Breaking Down User Stories**

  One of the core principles of Agile is to work incrementally and iteratively. Estimation aids this process by identifying the need to break down larger user stories into smaller, more manageable tasks. This breakdown not only makes the work more digestible but also allows teams to tackle complex projects systematically, ensuring consistency and quality in the development process.

- **Prioritizing the Product Backlog**

  Effective backlog management is key to successful Agile projects. Estimation plays a critical role in prioritizing the backlog, as it helps balance the perceived value of features against the effort required to deliver them. By understanding both the complexity involved and the potential impact on users, teams can make informed decisions about what to work on next, optimizing the value delivered in each iteration.

- **Planning Upcoming Work**

  Agile is dynamic, with plans evolving based on project progress and stakeholder feedback. Estimation provides a framework for this adaptability in short-term planning. By estimating tasks, teams can set realistic goals for upcoming sprints and manage expectations both within the team and with stakeholders. This planning ensures that the project moves forward in a structured yet flexible manner.

While estimation in Agile may not always predict exact outcomes, its real value lies in enhancing team communication, understanding the work, and effective planning. By embracing the true purpose of Agile estimation, teams can improve their workflow, prioritize effectively, and plan their work with greater confidence and flexibility.

The Pitfalls of Estimating in Hours

Estimating the time it takes to complete tasks in hours is a common practice, but it comes with several drawbacks:

- **Subjectivity and Variability**: Hourly estimates can be highly subjective, varying significantly depending on the individual's experience and speed. What might take one developer four hours could take another six, leading to inconsistencies and debates over the seniority and capabilities of team members.

- **Overlooking Obstacles**: When tasks are estimated purely in terms of time, potential obstacles and complexities might be overlooked. Developers might focus more on hitting the estimated hours rather than dealing with the actual complexity of the task, which can lead to technical shortcuts or incomplete implementations.

- **Reassignment Issues**: Hourly estimates are often tied to a specific developer's abilities. If a task needs to be reassigned to another developer, the original estimate may no longer be valid, which can disrupt project timelines and workload planning.

The Merits of Story Points

In contrast, estimating in story points offers a range of advantages that align more closely with Agile principles:

- **Focus on Relative Complexity**: Story points measure the complexity of a task relative to other tasks, not in absolute terms. This approach encourages teams to make comparisons based on a task's inherent difficulty, required resources, and potential risks, rather than just time.

- **Collective Wisdom**: When teams estimate with story points, they use their collective experience and understanding of the work. This collaborative approach helps build a more accurate picture of the task's demands, drawing on the diverse insights of the whole team.

- **Acknowledging Human Estimation Strengths**: Humans are generally better at making relative comparisons than absolute judgments. Story points leverage this cognitive strength, allowing teams to assess new user stories against those they have already completed, which can lead to more accurate estimations.

- **Scalability and Flexibility**: Story points are unitless, making them scalable and flexible across different teams and projects. They accommodate changes in team composition and prevent the common pitfalls of reassignments that often plague hour-based estimates.

Switching from hours to story points can transform the estimation process from a frequent source of stress into a strategic tool for planning and performance. By focusing on the relative complexity of tasks rather than the time they might take, teams can improve their project estimations and foster a more collaborative and flexible planning culture. This shift not only aligns with Agile methodologies but also enhances the overall productivity and morale of the development team.

The Dangers of Misusing Scrum Velocity

Despite its benefits, estimation can lead to challenges, particularly when misused as a tool for setting rigid deadlines or measuring individual team performance. Such practices can undermine the Agile principles of collaboration and flexibility, leading to stress and burnout among team members. It's important for Agile teams to understand that estimates are indicative and should be used to foster better planning and communication rather than as strict metrics for accountability.

Velocity, a metric used to measure the amount of work a team can tackle in a sprint, can be problematic. When used as a productivity measure, it can lead to "story points inflation," eroding trust, frustrating team members, and potentially harming the software quality (Figure 2-3). This misuse can occur even without bad intentions, as a natural response to pressure.

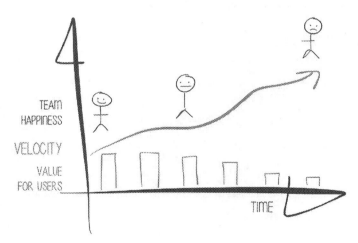

Figure 2-3. *Team happiness vs. velocity*

Metrics That Matter

Research shows that a significant portion of a developer's time is spent understanding code, with a smaller fraction on writing and other coding-related activities. These activities are difficult to quantify upfront. Therefore, in line with Agile principles, the focus should be on consistently delivering value. The ultimate metrics should be the value delivered and customer satisfaction, assessed by the quality and utility of the software rather than the speed or volume of work completed.

As we wrap up this section on estimation and planning within the Agile framework, it becomes apparent that while this practice is often met with skepticism, its strategic execution is fundamental for the success of Agile projects. Estimation in Agile is less about achieving precision in predictions and more about fostering understanding, facilitating planning, and guiding effective team collaboration.

Key Takeaways

- **Purpose of Estimation**: Agile estimation is crucial not for its accuracy in predicting the future, but for its role in facilitating a shared understanding of work scope, breaking down user stories, prioritizing backlogs, and planning upcoming work.

- **Beyond Hourly Estimates**: Estimating in hours often leads to inefficiencies and inaccuracies, primarily due to the variability in individual capabilities and unforeseen challenges. Shifting the focus from hours to story points offers a more flexible and relative measure of complexity and effort.

- **Value of Story Points**: Estimation using story points emphasizes relative sizing, encouraging teams to draw on collective experiences and understanding of task complexities. This approach is more aligned with human capabilities in assessing relative sizes rather than absolute terms.

- **Scrum Velocity with Caution**: While velocity can be a useful metric, its misuse as a productivity measure can lead to detrimental effects such as story points inflation. This not only erodes trust but can also compromise software quality and team morale.

- **Metrics That Truly Matter**: In Agile, the ultimate metrics are those that reflect value delivery and customer satisfaction. Assessing the quality and utility of the software, rather than merely the speed or volume of work completed, aligns more closely with Agile principles. It's important to recognize that significant aspects of software development, like understanding code, are not easily quantifiable but are critical to the project's success.

In conclusion, effective Agile estimation and planning require a shift in perspective from traditional methods. By focusing on relative sizing, understanding the real purpose of estimation, and valuing metrics that matter, Agile teams can enhance their planning processes and deliver greater value. This approach not only aligns with Agile principles but also ensures that projects are managed in a way that is responsive to change, focused on real progress, and geared toward delivering high-quality software.

Effective Meetings

Agile project management is highly iterative and values constant feedback to adapt and improve continuously. This dynamic environment requires frequent meetings to ensure that all stakeholders are informed and engaged. Effective meetings are crucial for the success of Agile projects, as they facilitate communication, planning, and decision-making. However, to avoid meetings becoming a drain on productivity, it is vital to conduct them efficiently. This section explores the types of Agile meetings and best practices for making them productive.

Types of Agile Meetings

- **Daily Stand-up Meetings**: These brief sessions are designed to update each team member on the project's progress and any immediate blockers. It is essential to keep the daily stand-up concise and focused. The use of an updated board during these meetings allows everyone to visually track progress and align on the day's objectives.

- **Backlog Refinement Meetings**: Prior to these meetings, pre-refinement should be done to assess and prepare the backlog items for discussion. This ensures that the time spent during the meeting is focused on discussing the specifics of each item to refine them further. The backlog should be prioritized before the meeting to streamline the discussion process.

- **Sprint Planning Meetings**: These meetings require clear goals and objectives from the leaders. The focus is on defining what to complete in the upcoming sprint and planning the workload accordingly. It's a collaborative session where team roles and responsibilities for the sprint are clarified.

- **Sprint Review Meetings**: At the end of each sprint, the team reviews the outcomes and deliverables. The aim is to demonstrate what has been accomplished during the sprint in a way that is understandable to all stakeholders, including non-technical ones. This meeting is crucial for gathering feedback and discussing what was achieved or what was left for the next sprint.

Best Practices for Agile Meetings

- **Streamlined Meetings**: Effective Agile meetings require preparation. Encourage team members to do necessary pre-work for the meetings, such as updating task boards or reviewing backlog items. This preparation ensures that the meeting time is used efficiently.

- **Facilitation and Documentation**: Each meeting should have a designated leader to facilitate the discussion and ensure that the meeting stays on track. This person is also responsible for taking notes and documenting decisions and action items, which are critical for accountability and follow-up.

- **Creating a Safe Environment**: It is essential that all meetings provide a safe environment where team members feel comfortable providing honest feedback and collaborating fully. Encouraging openness and respect in discussions fosters a more cohesive team and a more productive meeting outcome.

- **Clear Goals and Objectives**: Particularly in planning and review meetings, it is crucial that the objectives of the meeting are clearly defined beforehand. This clarity helps in focusing the discussion and ensuring that all participants understand the meeting's purpose.

Effective meetings are a cornerstone of Agile project management, enabling teams to stay aligned, informed, and responsive to changes. By adhering to these practices and continuously seeking ways to improve the efficiency of meetings, Agile teams can ensure that these interactions are valuable and contribute positively to the project's progress. Regularly revisiting and refining meeting practices in response to team feedback is also vital for maintaining the relevance and effectiveness of these gatherings.

Conclusion

Drawing this chapter to a close, we've journeyed through the multifaceted world of Agile project management—a realm where adaptability, responsiveness, and customer-centric development reign supreme. From the foundational Agile Manifesto that revolutionized software development, to the nuanced practices of Scrum, Kanban, and Scrumban, we have unpacked the principles and values that underpin effective project management in the digital age.

Key Takeaways

- **Core Agile Principles**: The Agile Manifesto isn't just a set of ideals but a practical guide that has proven its relevance and vitality in modern software development. Embracing these values and principles ensures that project management processes are continuously aligned with the goals of efficiency and customer satisfaction.

- **Iterative Development and Continuous Delivery**: By breaking down the development process into manageable increments, Agile methodologies allow for constant evaluation and adaptation of the product, ensuring that the final deliverable meets user needs and adapts to changing market demands.

- **Frequent Feedback Loops**: Agile emphasis on regular feedback ensures that the development process is aligned with customer expectations and project goals, reducing the risks of significant project deviations and increasing the product's market relevance.

- **Understanding and Applying Scrum and Kanban**: While both frameworks fall under the Agile umbrella, they cater to different project management needs. Scrum, with its structured sprints and roles, is suited to projects requiring rigorous timelines, whereas Kanban offers more flexibility and is ideal for ongoing improvements.

- **Leveraging Scrumban**: This hybrid approach combines the structure of Scrum and the flexibility of Kanban, making it an excellent choice for projects that evolve in complexity and scope. Transitioning from Scrum to Scrumban allows teams to grow their management strategies in parallel with project demands and team dynamics.

- **Ticket Management and Workflow**: Effective management of tickets, from Initiatives to Tasks, facilitates not only detailed planning but also clear communication of progress and expectations. This structured breakdown is essential for maintaining project oversight and ensuring all team members are aligned.

- **Agile Estimation Techniques**: Moving from traditional hour-based estimations to story points can significantly enhance the planning process by focusing on the complexity and effort involved rather than time. This shift helps prevent common pitfalls associated with under- or overestimating tasks based on time alone.

- **Conducting Effective Agile Meetings**: Meetings in an Agile setting are not just administrative check-ins but pivotal moments for collaboration, planning, and alignment. Best practices in conducting these meetings ensure they are productive and truly beneficial to the project's progression.

Agile project management offers more than just a methodology; it provides a framework for fostering a proactive, responsive, and highly collaborative team environment. By integrating the principles of Agile, focusing on effective ticket management, and adapting the approach to the nuances of each project, teams can achieve not just operational efficiency but also higher satisfaction and value delivery to customers. As we have seen, the key to successful Agile project management lies in understanding and thoughtfully applying its practices to fit the unique challenges and opportunities of each project.

CHAPTER 3

Elevating Code Quality

Quality code stands as the cornerstone of successful software development, embodying the principles of clarity, maintainability, and efficiency. It transcends mere functionality to ensure that software is built on a foundation that guarantees longevity, scalability, and ease of collaboration. This chapter delves into the essence of code quality, underscoring the significance of learning from industry veterans and the open source community to avoid reinventing the wheel and to sidestep the pitfalls of immature practices that pervade the software development landscape.

The investment in writing quality code yields dividends far beyond the immediate project at hand. It paves the way for future enhancements, simplifies maintenance, and facilitates a better understanding among developers who may interact with the codebase down the line. Quality code is a critical investment in the project's future and a reflection of the development team's professionalism and foresight.

At the heart of code quality are the principles and best practices that have been honed and shared within the open source community. These guidelines are the distillation of countless hours of trial and error, collaboration, and collective wisdom.

© The Editor(s) (if applicable) and The Author(s),
under exclusive license to APress Media, LLC, part of Springer Nature 2024
A. Souza, *Tech Leadership Playbook*, https://doi.org/10.1007/979-8-8688-0543-1_3

In the fast-paced and ever-evolving world of software development, the wisdom of learning from those who have trod the path before us cannot be overstated. Rather than reinventing the wheel with each new project, drawing from the vast reservoir of established guidelines, best practices and programming principles enables professionals to build on the collective knowledge and experience of the software development community.

The open source community, with its ethos of collaboration and transparency, serves as a rich repository of knowledge on effective programming practices. Engaging with this community and adopting its best practices not only enhances code quality but also fosters a culture of continuous learning and improvement among developers.

The maturity of a software developer is often gauged by their familiarity with and adherence to the community programming principles. It's a reflection of their ability to synthesize community wisdom with personal experience, resulting in solutions that are not just effective but also elegant and maintainable.

Despite the wealth of knowledge available, the software development industry remains marked by a prevalence of bad practices. This reality underscores the importance of continuous learning, critical evaluation of existing methods, and a commitment to adopting practices that have been vetted by the community for their efficacy.

In this chapter, we will delve into what constitutes quality code, the pivotal role of open source community best practices and programming principles. Through this exploration, we aim to equip developers with the tools and knowledge necessary to elevate their code and the software quality

Embracing Programming Principles for Effective Software Development

Programming principles are the cornerstone of good software development. They offer a framework that helps developers navigate the complexities of coding, ensuring that the software is built with clarity, efficiency, and a focus on future maintainability. Adhering to these principles reduces complexity, mitigates technical debt, and facilitates a smoother development process. It also aids in achieving a unified coding standard across the team, making the codebase more cohesive and understandable for every team member.

While the software development community recognizes a broad array of programming principles, it's essential for each team to identify and agree upon a subset that resonates with their specific project needs and team dynamics. Creating a programming principles document allows a team to formalize these selected guidelines, ensuring that every member is aligned and committed to these practices. This document serves as a reference point for current and future team members, encapsulating the team's approach to coding excellence.

Among the vast list of programming principles, a few stand out for their universal applicability and impact on software quality. Here are some of my favorites that every development team should consider including in their principles document:

- **KISS (Keep It Simple, Stupid)**: Advocates for simplicity in design and implementation, discouraging unnecessary complexity.

- **YAGNI (You Aren't Gonna Need It)**: Emphasizes avoiding the implementation of features or functionalities until they are truly needed.

- **Clean Code Over Clever Code**: Prioritizes readability and maintainability of code over showcasing technical acrobatics. The goal is to write code that is easily understood by others (and by you in the future).

- **Avoid Premature Optimization**: Warns against optimizing code before it's clear where bottlenecks actually exist, promoting the idea that first, code should be correct and readable.

- **Single Responsibility Principle**: Each module or class should have responsibility over a single part of the functionality provided by the software, and that responsibility should be entirely encapsulated by the class.

- **Composition Over Inheritance**: Encourages the use of composition to achieve code reuse and flexibility instead of relying heavily on inheritance.

- **Fail Fast, Fail Hard**: Suggests that systems should be designed to detect issues as early as possible in the development process, making them easier to address before they escalate.

Incorporating these principles into your team's programming ethos can significantly enhance the quality of your software projects. By understanding and applying these guidelines, developers can produce code that is not just functional but also elegant and future-proof.

Best Practices Documents: Cultivating Excellence in Software Development

In the complex and collaborative world of software development, establishing a shared understanding of how tasks should be approached and executed is paramount. One of the most effective tools for achieving this harmony is the creation and adoption of best practices documents. These documents serve as a beacon, guiding teams in maintaining high standards of work across various activities involved in software development.

Foundation and Refinement

The journey to crafting a comprehensive best practices document ideally begins with insights and guidelines already established by the broader software development community. This collective wisdom acts as a solid foundation, providing proven strategies and techniques that have been embraced by developers worldwide. However, the one-size-fits-all approach seldom applies perfectly to every team's unique context. Therefore, it is crucial for teams to refine these community-sourced guidelines, tailoring them to fit their specific project needs, team dynamics, and organizational culture. This customization process ensures that the best practices document resonates with the team's experience and aspirations, making it a more effective tool for guiding their work.

Streamlining Code Reviews

One of the tangible benefits of a well-established best practices document is its ability to streamline code review processes. By setting clear expectations for code quality, style, and structure, these documents significantly reduce the need for lengthy discussions during code reviews. Teams can reference the best practices as a checklist, ensuring that submissions adhere to agreed-upon standards before they even reach the review stage. This not only speeds up the review process but also enhances the overall quality of the codebase.

Examples of Best Practices Documents

For teams looking to develop their own best practices documents, numerous resources are available within the software development community. In the following, I provide two examples of best practices documents for your inspiration.

Logging Best Practices

Record events at the correct level:

- DEBUG—Used for debugging.

- INFO—Informs expected system operation.

- WARN—A recoverable problem occurred, but with no user experience impact.

- ERROR—An unrecoverable problem occurred, with some user experience impact.

- FATAL—Indicates fatal errors. Usually, it means the end of the program.

Best practices:

- Don't log sensitive information. Make sure you never log (Passwords, Credit card numbers, Social security numbers...).

- On error, log all the available information to reproduce the issue.

- When calling an external service, in case of error, log the request and response for the called service (exclude PII).

- When calling an external service, log the request and response for the called service as DEBUG (exclude PII).

- When the service fails to respond to a request, add the request-id as part of the error message response.

- Consider logging the service response data as DEBUG (Exclude PII).

- Consider logging the service request data as INFO (Exclude PII).

- Log bad request as a WARNING.

- Include the stack trace when logging exceptions.

- Include the thread's name when logging from a multithreaded application.

- Timestamps should be at millisecond resolution (YYYY-MM-DD HH:mm:ss.yyy).

- DateTime should be UTC.

- Logged durations should be milliseconds.

- Log in JSON format.

- An error should be handled only once. Logging an error is handling an error. So an error should either be logged or propagated(re throw), make sure you are handling it on the right layer/place.

- Enable log level change at runtime. You should be able to change the log level when troubleshooting in prod.

- Split logs of different levels to different targets to control their granularity. Even if using WARN as the production log level. The application start-up INFO should still be logged.

- Log all the important environment configuration info on start up. Ex. Service dependency URLs, server ports, etc.

Audit Best Practices

Where possible, always log:

- Input validation failures, for example, protocol violations, unacceptable encodings, invalid parameter names and values

- Output validation failures, for example, database record set mismatch, invalid data encoding

- Authentication successes and failures

- Authorization (access control) failures

- Session management failures, for example, cookie session identification value modification

- Application errors and system events, for example, syntax and runtime errors, connectivity problems, performance issues, third party service error messages, file system errors, file upload virus detection, configuration changes

- Application and related systems start-ups and shutdowns, and logging initialization (starting, stopping, or pausing)

- Use of higher-risk functionality, for example, network connections, addition or deletion of users, changes to privileges, assigning users to tokens, etc.

Code Review Best Practices

In doing a code review, you should make sure that:

- The code is well-designed.

- The functionality is good for the users of the code.

- Any UI changes are sensible and look good.

- Any parallel programming is done safely.

- The code isn't more complex than it needs to be.

- The developer isn't implementing things they might need in the future but doesn't know they need it now.

- The code has appropriate unit tests.

- Tests are well-designed.

- The developer used clear names for everything.

- Comments are clear and useful and mostly explain why instead of what.

- The code is appropriately documented.

- The code conforms to our style guides.

Make sure to review every line of code you've been asked to review, look at the context, make sure you're improving code health, and compliment developers on good things that they do.

How Fast Should Code Reviews Be?

If you are not in the middle of a focused task, you should do a code review shortly after it comes in.

One business day is the maximum time it should take to respond to a code review request (i.e., first thing the next morning).

Pull Request

- Create small PRs.

- Add the JIRA ticket to the PR title.

- Write descriptions with all information that will help the reviewers.

- Wait to merge the branch until continuous integration (TDDium, Travis CI, CircleCI, etc.) tells you the test suite is green in the branch.

- Always delete your branch after merging it.

- If not sharing your branch, use the squash option.

- One approval is required.

Code Review Ethics

When our code is being reviewed or when we review the work of others, it's essential to have the correct mindset to make it a positive experience and reap all the benefits of this effort.

Everyone

- Accept that many programming decisions are opinions. Discuss trade-offs, which you prefer, and resolve quickly.

- Ask good questions; don't make demands. ("What do you think about naming this :user_id?")

- Good questions avoid judgment and avoid assumptions about the author's perspective.

- Ask for clarification. ("I didn't understand. Can you clarify?")

- Avoid selective ownership of code. ("mine," "not mine," "yours")

- Avoid using terms that could be seen as referring to personal traits. ("dumb," "stupid"). Assume everyone is intelligent and well-meaning.

- Be explicit. Remember people don't always understand your intentions online.

- Be humble. ("I'm not sure—let's look it up.")

- Don't use hyperbole ("always," "never," "endlessly," "nothing").

- Don't use sarcasm.

- Keep it real. If emoji, animated gifs, or humor aren't you, don't force them. If they are, use them with aplomb.

- Talk synchronously (e.g., chat, screen-sharing, in-person) if there are too many "I didn't understand" or "Alternative solution:" comments. Post a follow-up comment summarizing the discussion.

Having Your Code Reviewed

- Be grateful for the reviewer's suggestions. ("Good call. I'll make that change.")

- A common axiom is "Don't take it personally. The review is of the code, not you." We used to include this, but now prefer to say what we mean: Be aware of how hard it is to convey emotion online and how easy it is to misinterpret feedback. If a review seems aggressive or angry or otherwise personal, consider if it is intended to be read that way and ask the person for clarification of intent, in person if possible.

- Keeping the previous point in mind: assume the best intention from the reviewer's comments.

- Explain why the code exists. ("It's like that because of these reasons. Would it be more clear if I rename this class/file/method/variable?")

- Push commits based on earlier rounds of feedback as isolated commits to the branch. Do not squash until the branch is ready to merge. Reviewers should be able to read individual updates based on their earlier feedback.

- Seek to understand the reviewer's perspective.

- Try to respond to every comment.

- Merge once you feel confident in the code and its impact on the project.

- Final editorial control rests with the pull request author.

Reviewing Code

Understand why the change is necessary (fixes a bug, improves the user experience, refactors the existing code). Then:

- Communicate which ideas you feel strongly about and those you don't.

- Identify ways to simplify the code while still solving the problem.

- If discussions turn too philosophical or academic, move the discussion offline to a regular Friday afternoon technique discussion. In the meantime, let the author make the final decision on alternative implementations.

- Offer alternative implementations, but assume the author already considered them. ("What do you think about using a custom validator here?")

- Seek to understand the author's perspective.

- Remember that you are here to provide feedback, not to be a gatekeeper.

The core message of this section is clear: By embracing best practices documents, software development teams can enhance their efficiency, improve code quality, share knowledge and foster a culture of continuous improvement. These documents are living artifacts, evolving as the team grows and the project advances, ensuring that they remain relevant and valuable over time.

Enhancing Code Quality with Static Analysis Tools

In the quest for superior code quality, static analysis tools emerge as indispensable allies for developers. These tools scrutinize code without executing it, identifying potential errors, complexity issues, and deviations from best practices. This section delves into how developers can harness static analysis tools to not only improve code quality but also ensure adherence to architectural guidelines, reduce coupling, and enhance security.

Leveraging Static Analysis for Code Improvement

Static analysis tools offer a comprehensive way to assess code quality, providing insights that might be overlooked during manual reviews. By integrating these tools into the development workflow, teams can automate the detection of common issues, leading to more efficient and reliable code.

- **Measuring Code Complexity**: Tools that measure cyclomatic and cognitive complexity help developers understand how intricate their code is. Simplifying complex code not only makes it more maintainable but also reduces the risk of bugs. Cyclomatic complexity measures the number of linearly independent paths through a program's source code, while cognitive complexity assesses how difficult code is to understand for a human reader.

- **Ensuring Architectural Boundaries with Architecture Tests**: Static analysis can enforce architectural rules and boundaries, preventing erosion of the codebase structure. Architecture tests can verify layer dependencies, ensuring that high-level modules do not depend on low-level modules, and identify violations of predefined architectural patterns.

- **Preventing High Coupling and Broad Responsibility by Limiting Imports**: Tools can enforce limits on the number of imports a module or class can have, encouraging developers to adhere to the principle of single responsibility and promote low coupling. This facilitates a modular architecture where components can be easily tested, replaced, or updated.

- **Enforcing Single Responsibility Principle by Limiting Method Size**: To prevent methods from taking on too many responsibilities, static analysis tools can flag methods that exceed a certain length. This encourages developers to refactor large methods into smaller, more focused functions, enhancing code clarity and testability.

- **Preventing Security Issues**: Perhaps one of the most critical applications of static analysis is in identifying security vulnerabilities. Tools can detect common security flaws like SQL injection, cross-site scripting (XSS), and insecure dependencies, helping teams address these issues before they can be exploited.

Examples of Static Analysis Tools

Several static analysis tools are available for different programming languages and environments. Some popular examples include:

- **SonarQube**: Offers a comprehensive suite for inspecting code quality, detecting bugs, and security vulnerabilities.

- **ESLint**: A pluggable linting utility for JavaScript and JSX, helping to find and fix problems in JavaScript code.

- **Checkstyle**: Assists with code styling and conventions in Java codebases.

- **RuboCop**: A Ruby static code analyser, based on the community Ruby style guide.

Integrating Static Analysis into Development Workflow

To maximize the benefits of static analysis, integrate these tools into your Continuous Integration/Continuous Deployment (CI/CD) pipeline. This ensures that code is automatically analyzed with each commit, providing immediate feedback to developers and preventing quality regressions.

In conclusion, Static analysis tools are a vital component of modern software development, offering an automated means to improve code quality, enforce coding standards, and identify security vulnerabilities. By leveraging these tools, development teams can achieve more maintainable, secure, and high-quality codebases, aligning with best practices and industry standards.

The Critical Role of Code Review in Enhancing Code Quality

In the realm of software development, code review stands out not just as a practice but as a process to fostering code quality and consistency. Its benefits extend beyond mere error detection, encompassing knowledge sharing, mentoring, and the reinforcement of coding standards and best practices. This section delves into how code review, when effectively implemented, becomes an invaluable tool for software teams aiming to elevate the quality of their codebase.

Mentoring and Knowledge Sharing

One of the most significant benefits of code review is its role in the ongoing education and mentoring of developers. It provides a platform for more experienced developers to share insights on programming languages, frameworks, and software design principles with their peers. Leaving comments that introduce a developer to new concepts or techniques not only enriches their skill set but also contributes to the collective knowledge within the team. This practice of knowledge sharing through code review is instrumental in improving the overall health and maintainability of the codebase over time.

Automated Tools and Best Practices Documentation

For code review to be truly effective, it is essential that teams establish a foundation of code quality and consistency through automated tools and well-documented best practices. Automation plays a pivotal role in ensuring that code submissions meet basic standards before they even reach the review stage. Tools like linters, static analysis software, and automated tests can catch a wide array of common issues, from syntax errors to more subtle logical errors, thereby streamlining the review process.

Equally important is the existence of a best practices document. Such a document outlines the coding standards and methodologies endorsed by the team, providing clear guidance on expectations regarding code quality. It ensures that all team members, regardless of their experience level, understand what constitutes acceptable code within the project. This clarity allows reviewers to focus more on evaluating the business logic and architectural decisions rather than correcting basic syntax or style issues.

Concentration on Business Logic

With automated tools handling the enforcement of coding standards and a best practices document guiding coding methodologies, reviewers can dedicate their attention to the more nuanced aspects of the code under review. They can concentrate on assessing the business logic, ensuring that it is sound, efficient, and aligned with the project's objectives.

This focus on the core functionality of the code, rather than surface-level issues, not only enhances the quality of the review process but also fosters a culture of thoughtful and constructive feedback.

The Significance of a Code Review Best Practices Document

In addition to leveraging automated tools and a comprehensive best practices document for coding, the establishment of a code review best practices document is equally crucial. This document serves as a guideline for conducting effective and efficient code reviews, setting the standard for what is expected in the review process. It outlines how to provide constructive feedback, prioritize issues, and maintain a respectful and collaborative review environment. By having clear guidelines, teams can avoid common pitfalls such as unproductive criticism or focusing too much on trivial matters, ensuring that the code review process is not only about critiquing code but also about fostering a culture of continuous improvement and mutual respect.

In summary, code review is a multifaceted process with the power to significantly impact code quality, team knowledge, and project success. By combining the strengths of mentoring, automated tools, and a solid foundation of coding best practices, teams can leverage code review as a means to not only catch errors but also educate developers, enforce consistency, and ensure that business logic is robust and effective. Embracing code review as a critical component of the software development life cycle is a step toward building more reliable, maintainable, and high-quality software systems.

Technical Debt: A Strategic Perspective

Technical debt is an intrinsic part of software development, a term that conjures images of quick hacks and suboptimal solutions. However, it's a nuanced concept that goes beyond the boundaries of expedient delivery or coding proficiency. In this section, we'll dispel some myths about technical debt, understand its inevitable accumulation, and explore strategies for managing it effectively.

The Inevitable Accumulation of Technical Debt

Technical debt accumulates not necessarily through negligence or poor practices but as a by-product of the software development process itself. It manifests when we code with partial knowledge of the problem domain, making assumptions that may later prove inadequate as our understanding evolves. This is not a reflection of the development team's skill but rather the reality of working within an ever-changing landscape where complete foresight is impossible.

Misconceptions and Realities

The common misconception is that technical debt arises solely from a rush to deliver or from inexperienced coding. However, even the most experienced teams following rigorous best practices can accrue technical debt. Why? Because it is not only the result of expedient choices but also an inherent outcome of dealing with uncertainty and the incomplete understanding that characterizes early stages of development.

There's a temptation to believe that investing more time in the design phase can prevent technical debt. While thorough design is crucial, it's not possible to anticipate every aspect of the application or the shifts in technology and business requirements that the future holds. The pursuit of a perfect design upfront can lead to analysis paralysis and delay the valuable learning that comes from implementation and real-world feedback.

Embracing a Leaner Cycle

A more practical approach is to embrace a lean cycle of development. By interleaving design, implementation, and refactoring phases, teams can create a continuous loop of learning and improvement. After implementing a set of functionalities, a deliberate refactoring phase allows consolidation of what has been built, ensuring that the codebase remains healthy and adaptable.

In this iterative process, the creation of technical debt is acknowledged and managed proactively. It's akin to taking out a loan: with the intention and capability to repay it promptly.

Managing Technical Debt Wisely

Technical debt, much like financial debt, isn't inherently harmful. It can be a strategic tool to achieve early market presence or handle temporary technical constraints. The key is to manage it judiciously. Teams should be aware of the debt they're incurring, making conscious decisions about when and where to allow it. Just as important is the plan to address it through refactoring and design improvements as more is learned about the system's requirements and as the product matures.

Conclusion

As we reach the end of this chapter on Code Quality, we reflect on the fundamental truth that quality is not an act but a habit. Through embracing programming principles and best practices, we set a solid foundation for excellence in software development. From establishing best practices documents to streamlining code reviews, we've seen how each element plays a vital role in cultivating a culture of quality.

Key Takeaways

- **Programming Principles for Effective Development**: Principles like KISS, YAGNI, and the Single Responsibility Principle serve as the backbone for writing maintainable and understandable code. Emphasizing simplicity and responsibility in code design ensures that systems are both robust and adaptable to change.

- **Establishment of Best Practices**: Documenting and disseminating best practices, such as those for logging and code reviews, help cultivate a shared understanding among team members. This shared understanding is crucial for maintaining consistency and excellence in software development across diverse teams and projects.

- **Utilization of Static Analysis Tools**: Static analysis tools are invaluable for consistently measuring code quality and enforcing project-specific guidelines. By integrating these tools into the development workflow, teams can proactively address issues like code complexity, architectural integrity, and security vulnerabilities.

- **Integrating Static Analysis into Workflow**: The integration of static analysis tools into the development cycle allows for continuous feedback and improvement, making code quality a central aspect of the development process rather than an afterthought.

- **The Role of Code Review**: Code reviews are critical for team collaboration and quality assurance. They provide a platform for sharing knowledge, catching errors early, and collectively pushing toward higher standards.

- **Technical Debt Management**: Understanding and managing technical debt is crucial for long-term project health. Recognizing when to take on debt strategically and when to pay it down is a skill that can significantly enhance the sustainability of software projects.

- **Adopting a Leaner Development Cycle**: Embracing lean principles in software development can help teams minimize waste, accelerate delivery, and focus on creating value through high-quality software.

Enhancing code quality is not merely about adhering to technical norms but about fostering a culture that values quality in every line of code. The principles, practices, and tools discussed in this chapter are not just guidelines but essential components of a robust development ecosystem. They enable developers to not only tackle current projects with efficiency but also to build a foundation that anticipates and adapts to future challenges and technologies.

CHAPTER 4

Software Design and Architecture

Software design and architecture stand as pillars in the creation of robust, scalable, and maintainable software systems. These disciplines, vast in scope and rich in detail, shape the foundation upon which all successful software projects are built. This chapter acknowledges the breadth of the subject and, with a pragmatic approach, aims to distill practical and critical insights for new projects or teams venturing into the architectural realm of software development.

This chapter provides an overview of key concepts in software design and architecture, focusing on practical insights and essential tips beneficial for new projects or teams. It aims to present foundational knowledge in a structured manner, highlighting the importance of understanding and applying core architectural principles.

Topics covered include:

- **Boundaries**: The significance of establishing clear component boundaries within a system for improved modularity and flexibility

- **Code Structure Strategies**: Discussion on horizontal vs. vertical code structure, and their implications for project organization and development efficiency

A. Souza, *Tech Leadership Playbook*, https://doi.org/10.1007/979-8-8688-0543-1_4

- **Architectural Styles**: A comparison of monolithic and microservices architectures, providing guidance on selecting the most appropriate style based on project requirements

The chapter is designed to equip readers with a solid understanding of fundamental software architecture concepts, enabling informed decision-making in the design and development process.

The Pillars of Software Architecture

Software architecture is not just about choosing between microservices or monoliths, nor is it confined to the realms of Domain-Driven Design (DDD) or specific design patterns. Instead, it's grounded in the mastery of four pivotal concepts: coupling, cohesion, boundaries, and communication. Let's explore each:

- **Lower Coupling**: Coupling refers to the degree of interdependence between software components. Lower coupling ensures that changes in one component have minimal impact on others, facilitating easier maintenance and enhancing the system's adaptability to change. Achieving lower coupling means designing components that interact with each other through well-defined interfaces, minimizing direct knowledge of each other's inner workings.

- **Higher Cohesion**: Cohesion measures how closely related and focused the functionalities within a component are. Higher cohesion within components means that each component is dedicated to a specific task or functionality, without unnecessary overlap or dispersion of related functions across multiple components. This focus enhances the clarity and efficiency of the system, making it more intuitive to understand and work with.

- **Boundaries**: Defining clear boundaries between components is essential in delineating responsibilities and areas of concern within the system. Boundaries separate components, ensuring that they can operate independently and be developed, tested, and sometimes, deployed in isolation. They serve as the architecture's framework, dictating how components are divided and interact, and are crucial for enforcing both lower coupling and higher cohesion.

- **Communication Across Boundaries**: How components communicate across these boundaries is vital for the system's overall functionality and performance. Effective communication mechanisms ensure that components can exchange data and functionality as needed, without compromising their independence or creating tight couplings. This involves choosing appropriate protocols, data formats, and interfaces that support seamless interaction while adhering to the principles of lower coupling and higher cohesion.

Horizontal vs. Vertical Code Design

In the realm of software architecture, the strategic separation of concerns plays a pivotal role in creating systems that are both scalable and maintainable. This separation can be approached through two primary dimensions: horizontal and vertical. Understanding the distinction between these two, along with their application, is fundamental for architects aiming to design robust systems.

Horizontal Separation: Layers of Responsibility

Horizontal separation, or layering, involves dividing a system into distinct layers or tiers, each responsible for a specific aspect of the system's functionality. This approach typically includes:

- **Presentation Layer**: The user interface and user experience components

- **Business Logic Layer**: The core computational logic, rules, and processes

- **Data Persistence Layer**: The storage mechanisms, databases, and data access layers

The key advantage of horizontal separation is the isolation of concerns (Figure 4-1). For instance, separating the main business logic from the persistence logic ensures that changes in the database do not necessitate alterations in the business rules or processes. This isolation grants flexibility, allowing for database changes without impacting the core business logic and vice versa.

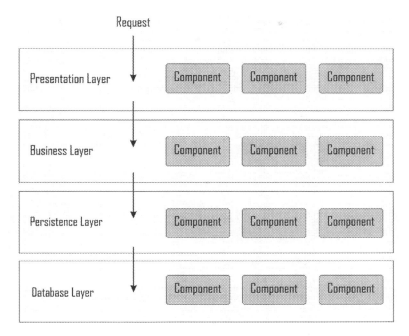

Figure 4-1. *Layers of responsibilities diagram*

Vertical Separation: Functional Segmentation

Vertical separation slices the system into functional segments, each dedicated to a distinct set of features or business capabilities, such as user management, product catalog, and checkout processes. This form of separation enables each segment to operate somewhat independently, focusing on its specific responsibilities.

An effective example of vertical separation is the delineation of different functional areas from each other (Figure 4-2). By maintaining low coupling (minimal dependencies between components) and high cohesion (related functionalities grouped together), the system benefits in several ways:

- **Scalability**: Each functional segment can be scaled independently, responding to specific demands without affecting the entirety of the system.

- **Maintainability:** Changes or updates within one segment have limited or no impact on others, simplifying maintenance efforts.

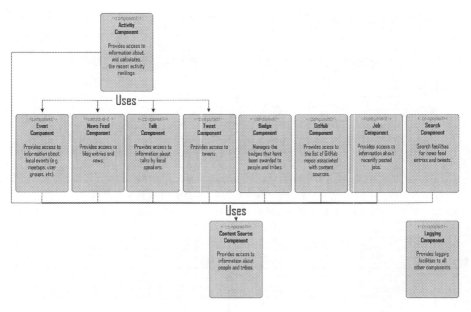

Figure 4-2. *Domain components*

In conclusion, the strategic decisions of implementing horizontal and vertical separation within software architecture are not just theoretical exercises; they are practical necessities for building scalable and maintainable systems. Horizontal separation ensures that changes in technology or design in one layer minimally impact others, while vertical separation allows for focused development on distinct system's functionalities. Together, these strategies enable the construction of complex systems that are easier to manage, evolve, and scale. Understanding and applying these concepts allow development teams to work more efficiently and adapt more readily to changing requirements or technologies.

Advocating for Vertical Separation

In the pursuit of enhanced cohesion and well-defined domain boundaries, I strongly advocate for teams to embrace vertical separation in their architectural approach. Vertical separation involves organizing the codebase into distinct segments or modules, each dedicated to a specific domain or functionality, such as User Management, Product Catalog, or Checkout Process (Figure 4-2). This method stands in contrast to horizontal separation, which layers the codebase according to technical roles like presentation, business logic, and data access (Figure 4-1).

Why Vertical Separation?

Vertical separation brings numerous benefits that align with our goals for a clean, maintainable, and scalable architecture:

- **Enhanced Cohesion**: By keeping all aspects of a domain within a single vertical slice, we ensure that related functionalities stay together. This not only simplifies understanding and development within that domain but also naturally promotes higher cohesion.

- **Well-defined Domain Boundaries**: Vertical separation makes the boundaries between different domains and functionalities explicit. Each vertical slice acts as a self-contained unit with its own responsibilities, reducing dependencies on other parts of the system. This clarity in domain boundaries is crucial for maintaining modular and flexible codebases.

- **Facilitates Scalability**: With domains encapsulated within distinct verticals, scaling becomes more manageable. Teams can focus on scaling or optimizing individual domains based on their specific requirements without impacting the broader system.

93

- **Encourages Domain-driven Design**: This approach aligns well with domain-driven design principles, encouraging teams to think in terms of business capabilities and domain logic, rather than technical layers. It fosters a deeper understanding of the business problems being solved and how the software architecture supports these goals.

Implementing Vertical Separation

To effectively implement vertical separation, teams should start by identifying the core domains or functionalities their system needs to address. From there, organizing the codebase into vertical modules that encapsulate all aspects of each domain—**from the user facing API down to data persistence**—sets a solid foundation for a cohesive and well-structured system.

Adopting vertical separation doesn't preclude the use of horizontal layers within each vertical module; rather, it reframes how we think about structuring our code. It encourages us to prioritize business logic and domain needs over technical categorization, leading to software that is more aligned with business objectives and easier to adapt and extend.

By following vertical separation, teams can achieve a balance of low coupling and high cohesion, facilitating a development environment where changes are localized, impact is clear, and the overall health of the codebase is preserved.

Clean Architecture

Clean Architecture, as proposed by Robert C. Martin (often referred to as Uncle Bob), advocates for a form of horizontal separation of concerns. The idea behind Clean Architecture (Figure 4-3) is to structure the system into layers with clear responsibilities, thereby decoupling the business logic from the UI, database, and external interfaces. Clean Architecture is typically illustrated as concentric circles, each representing a layer of the software.

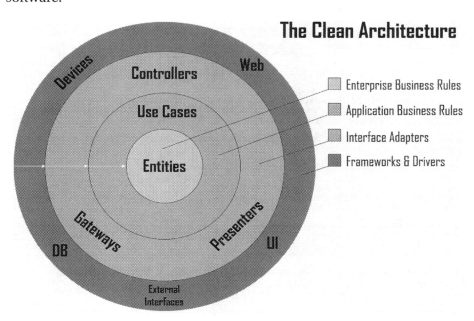

Figure 4-3. *Clean Architecture diagram*

- **Entities**: At the centre, entities encapsulate the enterprise-wide business rules. These are the business objects of the application.

- **Use Cases**: Surrounding the entities are the use cases, which contain application-specific business rules. These use cases orchestrate the flow of data to and from the entities and direct those entities to use their enterprise-wide business rules to achieve the goals of the use case.

- **Interface Adapters**: This layer contains adapters that convert data from the format most convenient for the use cases and entities, to the format most convenient for some external agency such as the Database or the Web. It is in this layer that the MVC (Model-View-Controller) structure typically lives.

- **Frameworks and Drivers**: The outermost layer is made up of frameworks and tools such as the Database, the Web Framework, etc. Ideally, this layer is kept to a minimum and is used as a way to glue the application to the outside world, with the inner layers being agnostic to the specific implementations of the external layers.

The horizontal separation in Clean Architecture refers to the separation of these layers across the application, with the dependency rule stating that inner layers should not depend on outer layers. This means that the business logic (entities and use cases) should not depend on the UI, frameworks, or any external element. Instead, dependencies should point inward, and outer layers should implement interfaces defined by the inner layers. This arrangement allows for a decoupled architecture where core logic is isolated from external concerns, supposedly facilitating easier testing and maintenance.

Clean Architecture is a powerful tool for designing and building software systems, particularly complex ones that require long-term maintenance and evolution. However, it's essential to weigh its benefits against the potential drawbacks and consider the specific needs of the project, including size, complexity, team expertise, and performance requirements, before adopting it. Most of the time, a simpler architectural style might be more appropriate based on the project's context and constraints.

Structuring Code Effectively

How code is structured can significantly impact both the maintainability and scalability of applications. Traditional methods often involve organizing code into conventional groupings such as by type or functionality. However, as applications grow in complexity and size, these traditional structures can lead to issues such as tight coupling and reduced readability. This section explores advanced strategies for breaking free from conventional groupings and minimizing access to ensure maximum clarity and maintainability.

Breaking Free from Conventional Groupings

Traditionally, code is organized by type—models here, controllers there, and views somewhere else. While this approach might seem logical, it often leads to scattered codebases where related functionalities are not co-located, making the code harder to follow and manage. A more effective approach involves grouping by feature or domain. This method, often referred to as modular or domain-driven design, organizes code around business domains or features, thus keeping all related code in a single, discoverable location.

- **Feature-Based Structure**: Organize directories and files around specific features or business logic. For instance, instead of having separate directories for controllers, views, and models, have a single directory for each distinct feature like "InvoiceManagement" or "UserProfiles."

- **Advantages**: This approach makes the codebase more navigable as developers can easily find all code related to a specific feature in one place. It also enhances the modularity of the code, making it easier to scale and update.

Consider the unrelated nature of **ProductRepository** and **UserRepository**. Grouping them merely because they are repositories overlooks the distinct domain problems they solve. A more enlightened approach groups **ProductEntity**, **ProductService**, and **ProductRepository** based on their coupling and cohesion—they change together, they stay together. This encapsulation guards the domain knowledge and ensures that each component serves a single, focused purpose (Figure 4-4).

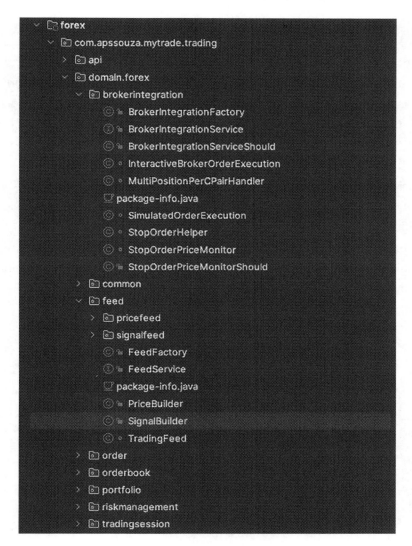

Figure 4-4. *Domain-driven code structure*

Minimizing Access for Maximum Clarity

Encapsulation is a fundamental concept in object-oriented programming that involves restricting direct access to some of an object's components, which can lead to increased security and robustness. By minimizing access to classes, methods, or variables, you not only protect the integrity of the data but also improve the understandability of the code by reducing its complexity.

A pivotal strategy in preventing your codebase from becoming a "big ball of mud" is restricting access levels. The liberal use of public access modifiers is a common pitfall; it invites unnecessary dependencies and entanglements. Instead, package your classes by domain/context, allowing interaction with other packages exclusively through well-defined interfaces (Figure 4-5). This discipline in access control is crucial for maintaining a clean, modular architecture.

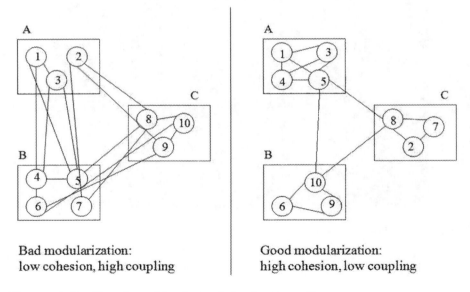

Bad modularization:
low cohesion, high coupling

Good modularization:
high cohesion, low coupling

Figure 4-5. *Good and bad modularization diagram*

Effective architecture is not just about decomposition into smaller components; it's about how these components interact within their bounded contexts. Clear boundaries are essential for maintaining domain integrity and ensuring components cooperate without undue reliance on one another. By breaking away from conventional groupings and minimizing access, developers can create more robust, secure, and clean applications. These practices not only improve the immediate readability and maintainability of code but also ensure that the application remains manageable as it scales.

Adopting these principles requires a shift in mindset from traditional methods, but the long-term benefits in terms of code quality and developer productivity are well worth the effort.

Practical Application: A Case Study

To illustrate these concepts, I embarked on an opensource project to design a monolithic application built on the foundations of modularity. This project serves as a practical example of how to apply the principles discussed, from domain-driven design to effective unit testing.

For a deeper dive into this project, including a walkthrough of its structure and the architectural decisions made, I invite you to check out the project and the accompanying video. This visual guide reinforces the lessons shared in this section and demonstrates how theoretical principles translate into real-world applications.

```
https://github.com/apssouza22/trading-system
```

Rethinking Domain Driven Design: Beyond Tactical Patterns

In recent years, Domain-Driven Design (DDD) has become a buzzword in the software development community, often surrounded by discussions focused on its tactical patterns: Entities, Value Objects, Repositories, Services, Aggregates, and more. This mainstream portrayal of DDD has, unfortunately, done a disservice to the software community. The emphasis on these complex patterns has led many to view DDD as overly complicated and inaccessible, particularly for projects that appear to have simpler domains.

The question arises: why entangle your project in the web of DDD's tactical patterns if they seem unnecessary?

The Misguided Focus and Its Consequences

The vast majority of content and discussions available online revolve around DDD's tactical aspects, obscuring its true essence and benefits. This skewed focus has made it easy to lose sight of what DDD fundamentally aims to achieve: the strategic advantage of clearly defined boundaries within your domain, encapsulated by the concept of a Bounded Context. Unfortunately, for many newcomers to DDD, the Bounded Context—the cornerstone of DDD's strategic patterns—is not what they first encounter. Instead, they are introduced to DDD through tutorials or sample applications that dive straight into its tactical patterns without establishing the foundational understanding of the domain itself.

Avoiding Dogmatic Adherence to DDD Tactics

It's crucial for teams not to fall into what could be termed "dogmatic DDD"—an unwavering focus on implementing DDD's tactical patterns without first grasping the strategic value of the methodology. While Entities, Aggregates, and Repositories, among other patterns, undoubtedly offer significant value, they should not precede the fundamental step of understanding and defining the domain through Bounded Contexts.

The Primacy of Bounded Contexts

A Bounded Context does more than just define the boundaries of a domain; it clarifies the domain's model and ensures that all team members share a common understanding of the domain's structure and language. This shared understanding is critical for effective communication and collaboration within the team and is often more valuable than the implementation of any specific pattern. While Bounded Contexts receive considerable attention from DDD enthusiasts, they should be the starting point for any team looking to adopt DDD, not an afterthought.

The essence of Domain-Driven Design lies not in the complexity of its tactical patterns but in the clarity and strategic insight it brings to software architecture through the definition of Bounded Contexts. By prioritizing a deep understanding of the domain and its boundaries, teams can leverage DDD to its full potential, applying tactical patterns where beneficial but not letting them overshadow the foundational principles of the methodology. In doing so, teams can demystify DDD, making it a powerful tool for tackling complexity in software projects, regardless of the perceived simplicity or complexity of their domain. The title says it all. It's not pattern-driven design, it's Domain-Driven Design

Architecture Testing: Ensuring System Integrity and Design Compliance

While functional testing verifies what a system does, architecture testing is critical to ensure how a system is structured and behaves under various scenarios. This section of the architecture chapter focuses on architecture testing, a crucial non-functional testing that ensures the software architecture adheres to predefined design principles and architectural rules. This testing is essential not only for maintaining the system's design integrity over time but also for ensuring that the system remains robust, scalable, and flexible.

Architecture testing is designed to validate the structural aspects of a system. It ensures that the system's architecture complies with the architectural patterns and principles that were initially designed. This form of testing is critical for

- **Preserving System Design**: It helps maintain the system's architectural blueprints and ensures that any deviations from the set architecture are identified early in the development process.

- **Enforcing Component Boundaries**: As systems evolve, maintaining clear component boundaries is crucial for modularity and flexibility. Architecture testing verifies that these boundaries are respected, which is essential for the system's long-term maintainability and scalability.

- **Adherence to Architectural Principles**: It ensures that the system conforms to the established architectural standards and principles, such as separation of concerns, layer dependencies, and service encapsulation.

To implement effective architecture testing, it is essential to use tools and frameworks that can automate the checking of architectural rules. Here's how architecture testing can be structured:

1. **Define Architectural Rules**: Establish clear rules that outline how different layers of the application interact with each other. This includes specifying allowable dependencies between layers and components.

2. **Automate Verification**: Use architectural testing tools to automate the verification of these rules. For instance, in Java-based applications, tools like ArchUnit can be employed to perform these checks programmatically.

Consider a Java application with a typical layered architecture comprising **Presentation**, **Service**, and **Persistence** layers. Using ArchUnit, we can define and enforce architectural constraints as follows:

```
JavaClasses jc = new ClassFileImporter().
importPackages("apssouza.engine");

LayeredArchitecture arch = layeredArchitecture()
    // Define layers
    .layer("Presentation").definedBy("..presentation..")
    .layer("Service").definedBy("..service..")
    .layer("Persistence").definedBy("..persistence..")
    // Add constraints
    .whereLayer("Presentation").mayNotBeAccessedByAnyLayer()
    .whereLayer("Service").mayOnlyBeAccessedByLayers
    ("Presentation")
    .whereLayer("Persistence").mayOnlyBeAccessedByLayers
    ("Service");

arch.check(jc);arch.check(jc);
```

In this example, the *LayeredArchitecture* construct is used to define each layer of the application and set rules about how these layers can interact. This ensures that layer dependencies are maintained as per the architectural design, preventing high-level modules from depending on lower-level modules directly.

Architecture testing is a vital practice in the software development life cycle, ensuring that the system's architecture remains clean and aligned with its design principles. By regularly performing architecture testing, developers can prevent significant architectural debt, ensuring that the system remains robust against changes and scalable for future enhancements. As part of the broader architectural considerations, this testing practice supports the overall health and performance of the software system, contributing to its success and longevity.

Leveraging Events and the Observer Pattern: A Double-Edged Sword

In the quest to reduce coupling within our software architectures, employing events and the observer pattern emerges as a potent strategy. This approach allows components to remain unaware of each other's existence while still enabling communication through the broadcasting of events and the subscription to these events by interested observers. It epitomizes the decoupling of components, as it eliminates the need for direct interaction between them. Here's how it achieves this:

- **Event-Driven Notifications**: Instead of one component calling another directly to pass data or trigger actions, the Observer pattern allows subjects to send notifications to registered observers whenever relevant events occur. This setup means that the subject does not need to know anything specific about the observers, other than that they implement a certain interface.

- **Independent Evolution**: Both subjects and observers can evolve independently of each other. A subject can change its internal state freely without worrying about how these changes are communicated to the observers. As long as it sends the notifications according to the agreed interface, any number of observers can be added or removed dynamically without impacting the subject.

The Benefits and Risks

Utilizing events and the observer pattern can significantly reduce coupling, making each component more independent and modular. This independence facilitates easier changes and additions to the system without affecting other parts, aligning well with the principles of a well-structured, maintainable codebase.

However, this reduction in coupling does not come without its trade-offs. The use of events and observers can introduce a new layer of complexity to the system. It can make the flow of control and data through the application harder to track, leading to potential challenges in debugging and understanding the system as a whole. The asynchronous nature of event handling can also introduce timing issues and make the execution flow less predictable.

A Word of Caution for New Teams

Given these complexities, while events and the observer pattern are powerful tools in the software architect's toolkit, they should be used with caution, especially by new teams or in projects at their inception. For most cases, particularly in environments where the team is still grappling with domain complexities and architectural best practices, introducing this level of indirection might not be advisable.

New teams might benefit more from simpler, more direct forms of component interaction that are easier to understand and debug. As the team matures and becomes more comfortable with the domain and the architecture, gradually introducing more advanced patterns like events and observers can be considered, always with a keen eye on maintaining system clarity and manageability.

Strategic Use for Maximum Benefit

When considering employing events and the observer pattern, it's crucial to weigh the benefits of reduced coupling against the potential increase in complexity. Use these patterns strategically, in parts of the system where the decoupling benefits outweigh the complexity costs, and always ensure that the team has the tools and knowledge necessary to manage the additional complexity introduced.

Reactive Programming in Software Design

Reactive programming is a paradigm tailored toward building systems that are more responsive, resilient, and scalable. This section will delve into the essence of reactive programming, discuss the synchronous issues it addresses, especially in the context of scalability and resource efficiency, and weigh its advantages and disadvantages. Given the evolution of modern programming technologies, such as lightweight concurrency, we'll also discuss why developers might consider alternatives to reactive programming.

What Is Reactive Programming?

Reactive Programming is a programming paradigm oriented around data flows and the propagation of change. It emphasizes writing code that reacts to changes, which can be anything from user interactions to incoming data from network requests. This paradigm is particularly suited for applications that need to handle a multitude of asynchronous events without blocking or waiting for these events to complete. By enabling non-blocking, event-driven programming, reactive programming can efficiently process operations with fewer threads, reducing overhead and enhancing scalability.

Key Concepts of Reactive Programming

1. **Asynchronous Data Streams**: At the core of Reactive Programming is the concept of streams. A stream is a sequence of ongoing events ordered in time. These can emit three different things: a value (of some type), an error, or a "completed" signal.

2. **Observables**: The main abstraction in Reactive Programming is the Observable. Observables help manage asynchronous data streams by acting as the data producer. In many reactive libraries (like RxJava, RxJS, etc.), Observables are used to create streams, transform them, combine them, or react to their emissions.

3. **Observers**: Observers subscribe to Observables to consume their values. An Observer typically reacts to three types of notifications: value emissions, an error, or completion of the stream. By subscribing, observers "listen" to the stream and react accordingly, which can include updating the UI, processing data, etc.

4. **Operators**: Reactive libraries provide operators that help you deal with streams in a declarative manner (such as map, filter, reduce, etc.). These operators can transform streams into new streams, for example, by changing each output of the stream with a function, filtering streams based on a condition, or merging multiple streams into one.

5. **Backpressure**: This is a mechanism for coping with streams that emit values faster than their observers can consume them. Reactive Programming provides ways to handle backpressure gracefully, ensuring that systems do not crash or lose data due to overflowing stream buffers.

Synchronous Issues and Scalability Challenges

Traditional synchronous processing often relies on blocking operations, especially during I/O operations like network or disk access. This results in inefficient resource utilization:

- **Thread Costs and System Resources**: Each blocking call typically ties up a system thread. Given that threads are relatively heavyweight in terms of system resources, excessive thread usage can lead to significant overhead.

- **Context Switching**: Frequent context switching, necessary when managing multiple threads, adds additional overhead. This switching is costly as it involves saving the state of one thread and loading the state of another, which can degrade performance, especially under high load.

Reactive programming addresses these inefficiencies by adopting an asynchronous, non-blocking approach that allows handling more operations with fewer threads and minimal context switching.

Consider a web application that needs to handle user inputs, API calls, and other I/O operations smoothly. With Reactive Programming, all these inputs are treated as asynchronous streams. The application can merge these streams, apply transformations, and subscribe to them with full support for backpressure and error handling, ensuring the application remains responsive and maintainable.

Reactive programming solves key issues in application scalability and responsiveness, making it especially suitable for:

- **Efficient Resource Utilization**: Minimizes the number of active system threads required and reduces the costs associated with context switching.

- **Handling High Throughput and Low Latency**: Ideal for applications that require managing a high volume of concurrent operations without compromising response times.

Pros of Reactive Programming

1. **Improved Responsiveness and Scalability**: Reactive systems are non-blocking and event-driven, allowing them to handle more concurrent users and operations with fewer resources compared to traditional blocking models. This leads to better responsiveness and scalability, particularly under load.

2. **Better Resource Utilization**: By avoiding thread blocking and efficiently handling asynchronous operations, Reactive Programming can make better use of system resources, such as CPU and memory, which is crucial in environments with limited resources.

3. **Simplified Error Handling and Increased Resilience**: Reactive Programming treats errors as first-class citizens of data streams, allowing errors to be managed declaratively and propagated through the stream's operators. This approach enhances system resilience by enabling comprehensive error recovery mechanisms.

4. **Enhanced Data Stream Management**: The ability to easily transform, combine, and react to asynchronous data streams in real time is a significant advantage. It provides a powerful abstraction that simplifies complex data handling tasks inherent in modern applications.

Cons of Reactive Programming

1. **Complexity in Understanding and Debugging**: Reactive Programming introduces a different way of thinking that can be challenging for developers accustomed to imperative programming styles. The asynchronous nature also makes debugging more difficult, as stack traces can become harder to interpret.

2. **Steep Learning Curve**: Learning how to build and maintain reactive applications can be daunting due to its conceptual and operational differences from traditional programming models.

3. **Overhead of Abstractions**: The abstractions provided by Reactive Programming, while powerful, can introduce overhead that may not be necessary for simpler applications where traditional approaches could suffice.

4. **Potential for Overuse**: Because of its powerful capabilities, there is a risk of overusing Reactive Programming for problems that do not require its sophisticated mechanisms, leading to unnecessarily complex solutions.

Justified Use Cases for Reactive Programming

The complexity of Reactive Programming is best justified in scenarios that require handling a large number of asynchronous events efficiently and robustly:

1. **API Gateways and Proxies**: In these systems, Reactive Programming can manage high volumes of concurrent requests and data flows efficiently. API gateways often act as the intermediary between clients and services, needing to handle requests that involve complex query capabilities, multiple backend services, and dynamic routing—all in real time.

2. **Real-time Data Processing Systems**: Systems that require real-time data processing, such as financial trading platforms, IoT (Internet of Things) data streams, or real-time analytics, greatly benefit from Reactive Programming. The ability to process and react to streams of data in real-time is crucial in these contexts, where delays can lead to significant repercussions.

Recommendations for New Teams

Given these complexities, while reactive programming offers significant benefits, it should be used with caution, especially by new teams or in projects at their inception. For most cases, particularly in environments where the team is still grappling with domain complexities and architectural best practices, introducing this level of complexity might not be advisable.

While reactive programming provides numerous benefits, especially for specific high-concurrency applications, it may not always be the best solution given the modern capabilities of many programming languages. Languages like Java, Kotlin, and Go offer robust support for lightweight concurrency models that can efficiently handle asynchronous operations without the need for a full reactive model. Developers should consider these simpler, more traditional concurrency models before adopting reactive programming.

Moreover, for applications hitting performance limits due to multithreading, scaling out by deploying multiple instances of the application behind a load balancer often offers a more straightforward and resource-efficient solution than re-architecting the application to use reactive programming.

Reactive programming is a powerful tool in the software developer's arsenal, especially useful for applications with high demands on concurrency and where latency and throughput are critical. However, it's essential to evaluate the specific needs of your application and consider simpler, more traditional methods of concurrency and scaling before committing to the complexity of a reactive approach. The choice should be guided by practical requirements and the specific challenges faced by your application, balancing the trade-offs between complexity, performance, and maintainability.

Exploring Architectural Styles: Monolith vs. Microservices

The debate between monolithic and microservices architectures represents a critical decision point for teams. Monoliths, characterized by their unified and centralized structure, offer simplicity in deployment and development. In contrast, microservices architectures embrace a distributed approach, promoting flexibility and scalability at the cost of increased complexity in coordination and infrastructure. This chapter will delve into the merits and challenges of each, providing guidance to help teams choose the path that best aligns with their project goals and capabilities.

Navigating the Microservices Landscape

The shift from monolithic architectures to microservices has been one of the most significant trends in software development in recent years. Microservices promise scalability and flexibility, appealing to teams looking to scale their applications and operational capabilities. However, this architectural style comes with its own set of challenges and complexities. Let's explore the primary reasons for adopting microservices, their inherent challenges, and strategies for managing their complexity.

Reasons for Adopting Microservices: Scale and Flexibility

The decision to adopt microservices often stems from two main needs: the need to scale teams and the need to scale applications. By breaking down an application into smaller, independently deployable services, organizations can assign different teams to work on each service, potentially increasing development speed and agility. Similarly, individual services can be scaled independently, allowing for more efficient use of resources and improved performance where it's needed most.

But Do These Benefits Justify the Complexity?

While the advantages are clear, the complexity that comes with microservices cannot be underestimated:

- **Networking Challenges**: Unlike monolithic applications, where components communicate within the same process, microservices communicate over the network. This shift introduces latency, potential points of failure, and the complexity of handling network unreliability.

- **Infrastructure Overhead**: Adopting microservices often means embracing container orchestration platforms like Kubernetes (k8s), adding layers of complexity to deployment, scaling, and management processes.

- **Service Mesh for Communication and Observability**: To effectively manage communication and observability across microservices, professional architectures often leverage a service mesh. While service meshes provide critical capabilities, they introduce additional complexity and learning curves.

- **API Versioning and Backward Compatibility**: Managing API versioning and ensuring backward compatibility becomes more challenging with microservices. Changes in one service can impact consumers, necessitating careful coordination and slowing down the pace of changes.

- **Embracing Duplication**: The microservices philosophy recommends avoiding shared libraries to minimize coupling. This approach often leads to code duplication across services, contrary to traditional software development practices that aim to minimize redundancy.

- **Monorepo vs. Poly-repo**: Contrary to the initial inclination toward poly-repo (separate repositories for each service) for microservices, managing microservices in a monorepo can simplify dependencies and shared code management, offering a more cohesive view of the entire ecosystem.

The core message of this section is clear: microservices architecture offers significant advantages for scalability and flexibility but comes at the cost of increased complexity. Before embarking on a microservices journey, teams must carefully weigh these benefits against the challenges of networking, infrastructure overhead, service communication, API management, and code duplication. Adopting strategies such as leveraging service meshes, considering monorepo approaches, and accepting certain levels of duplication can help manage some of the complexities. However, the decision to go down the microservices path should be made with a full understanding of the implications and a clear strategy for addressing the inherent challenges.

Embracing the Modular Monolith

In the debate between monoliths and microservices, a middle ground often combines the simplicity and cohesion of a monolith with the flexibility and scalability of microservices: the Modular Monolith (Figure 4-6). This approach adheres to the architectural boundaries discussed earlier, ensuring that the application is not just a single, intertwined codebase but a collection of isolated domain modules. Let's explore how a modular monolith addresses common development challenges while setting the stage for potential future evolution into microservices.

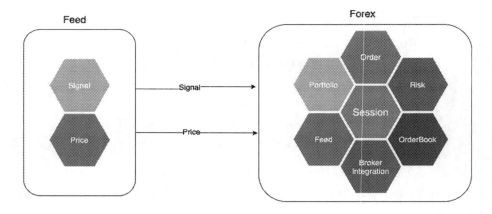

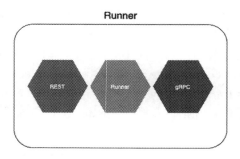

Figure 4-6. *Architetural boundaries diagram*

Architectural Boundaries within a Monolith

A monolithic application, by definition, might seem to advocate for a unified code structure. However, applying the principles of modular design within a monolith can significantly enhance maintainability and scalability. Each domain within the application should be encapsulated in its module, with clear boundaries that define its scope and interactions. This separation allows for

- **Improved Build Times**: By isolating domains into modules, changes in one area necessitate rebuilding only the affected module, not the entire application.

- **Clear Team Ownership**: Modules can be assigned to specific teams, clarifying responsibility and streamlining development processes.

- **Enhanced Automated Testing**: Isolated modules simplify the creation of automated tests by limiting the scope that each test needs to cover.

An example of this in the Java ecosystem is the use of Maven's multi-module projects, which enable developers to structure their monolith into clearly defined, independently buildable modules.

Scalability and Evolution

One of the standout features of a modular monolith is its inherent readiness for scalability. Should the need arise to scale a particular domain of the application, converting its corresponding module into a microservice is as straightforward as adding an API layer on top of it. This flexibility allows businesses to start with the simplicity of a monolith while retaining the option to scale into microservices as their needs evolve, without committing to a full microservices architecture from the outset.

Leveraging IDE Capabilities

A modular monolith also capitalizes on the integrated development environment (IDE) capabilities, facilitating safe, application-wide changes. The IDE's refactoring tools, code navigation, and other helpful features become more powerful when they can be applied across a well-organized, modular codebase. This accessibility encourages developers to make broader, more confident changes, knowing that the modular structure supports both the isolation and integration of changes across the application.

The Modular Monolith presents a compelling architecture model that balances the benefits of a monolithic application with the adaptability and scalability of microservices. By adhering to strict architectural boundaries and isolating domain modules, developers can enjoy the efficiencies of a monolith while preparing for the potential modularization into microservices. This approach not only facilitates practical aspects like build times and testing but also aligns with strategic goals for scalability and team collaboration. As such, the modular monolith stands as a robust foundation for both current and future software development needs.

To illustrate these concepts, check my, previously mentioned, opensource project. This project serves as a practical example of how to apply the principles discussed.

Embracing Service Mesh in Microservices Architecture

As software architecture evolves toward more distributed and decoupled systems, managing the complexities of communication and reliability between services becomes a critical challenge. If you are venturing down the path of microservices, one technology that deserves consideration is the service mesh. This section explores what a service mesh is, why it's beneficial, and how it works to streamline service-to-service communications in a microservices architecture.

What is a Service Mesh?

A service mesh is a dedicated infrastructure layer built to handle inter-service communications. It ensures that communication between service instances is fast, reliable, and secure. Service meshes are designed to handle a high volume of service-to-service traffic and provide critical capabilities such as service discovery, load balancing, encryption, authentication, and authorization transparently.

Why Consider Using a Service Mesh?

In microservices architectures, each service typically communicates with numerous other services. Managing this inter-service communication efficiently and securely can become overwhelmingly complex. A service mesh addresses these challenges by

- **Decoupling Communication from Application Logic**: By removing the need for services to manage communication logic, developers can focus on business logic. This separation simplifies development and maintenance of services.

- **Consistent Implementation of Cross-cutting Concerns**: Implementing requirements like security, observability, and resilience consistently across all services can be challenging. A service mesh provides these as built-in services that are uniform across the architecture, regardless of the service implementation technology.

- **Enhanced Observability and Reliability**: Service meshes offer sophisticated monitoring and tracing tools that help observe and diagnose issues in communications across services. They also improve system reliability with features like circuit breakers and timeouts.

Service-to-Service Communication via Sidecars

One of the pivotal concepts in a service mesh is the use of sidecars. A sidecar is a helper container that runs alongside each service instance, as part of the same Kubernetes pod, in a typical deployment:

- **Sidecar Pattern**: Each service in the mesh has a sidecar proxy that intercepts all incoming and outgoing network traffic. This pattern allows the service mesh to manage all aspects of the service's communications without any changes to the service's code.

- **Handling Communication Challenges**: Sidecars take over functionalities such as service discovery, load balancing, failure recovery, metrics, and monitoring, and even complex operational requirements like A/B testing, canary releases, rate limiting, and access control policies.

- **Infrastructure Layer Integration**: By integrating these functionalities at the infrastructure layer, rather than within the services themselves, the system gains performance improvements and better resource utilization. This setup also allows for dynamic routing and policy enforcement that can adapt to changing operational conditions without redeployment.

Implementing a service mesh can significantly ease the management of inter-service communications in microservices architectures, providing robust, scalable, and flexible communication infrastructure. It abstracts common challenges associated with microservices, such as fault tolerance and dynamic routing, away from application logic into the infrastructure layer. By doing so, it allows developers to focus more on delivering business value rather than the intricacies of network communication and reliability. Whether you are just starting with microservices or looking to optimize an existing system, considering a service mesh could be crucial to achieving operational excellence and architectural simplicity.

Conclusion

As we conclude our exploration of software design and architecture, we've journeyed through the fundamental principles that underpin robust, scalable, and maintainable systems. We've underscored the importance of adhering to key architectural principles such as lower coupling, higher cohesion, and the significance of well-defined boundaries. These principles are not mere theoretical concepts but essential guidelines that, when applied, can significantly enhance the quality and longevity of software systems. Whether through the lens of a modular monolith or the distributed nature of microservices, the core ideas of coupling, cohesion, boundaries, and communication serve as the foundation upon which decisions should be based.

Key Takeaways

1. **Emphasising Vertical Separation**: We discussed the significance of vertical over horizontal separation in code design, highlighting how this approach aligns with modern development practices that prioritize agility and scalability.

2. **Architecture Testing**: Testing isn't just for functionality—architecture testing plays a critical role in ensuring that the system adheres to its designed integrity and principles over time. This is essential for maintaining system reliability and performance under evolving requirements.

3. **Balancing Design Patterns**: The discussion on the Observer pattern revealed that while design patterns are powerful, they come with their own sets of benefits and risks. It is crucial to understand these fully to leverage patterns effectively without compromising the system's design and performance.

4. **Rethinking Domain-Driven Design (DDD)**: We moved beyond the tactical patterns of DDD to emphasize the strategic importance of bounded contexts, encouraging a thoughtful application of DDD that avoids dogmatic adherence and focuses on real-world effectiveness.

5. **Choosing the Right Architectural Style**: Whether debating between a monolith and microservices or considering the integration of a service mesh in microservices architecture, we recognized that the choice of architectural style should be driven by the specific needs and context of the project, rather than by prevailing trends alone.

6. **Modular Monolith as a Viable Option**: Before leaping into microservices, the modular monolith presents a compelling alternative, offering many of the benefits of microservices without some of the associated complexities. This option should not be overlooked in the quest for scalable and maintainable architectures.

Software architecture is as much an art as it is a science. As architects and developers, our goal should always be to design systems that not only meet the current needs but are also prepared for future challenges.

By embracing principles such as clean architecture, vertical separation, and strategic testing, and by being judicious in our application of design patterns and architectural styles, we can build software that is robust, flexible, and enduring.

This chapter has laid out a roadmap for navigating the complexities of modern software architecture. It encourages an informed, thoughtful approach to architectural decisions, advocating for a balance between innovation and practicality. As the field continues to evolve, so too should our strategies and methodologies, always with an eye toward sustainability and excellence in design.

CHAPTER 5

Product Quality Assurance

In the dynamic world of software development, the focus on product quality has become increasingly important. Quality Assurance (QA) acts as the custodian of this quality, making certain that software products not only fulfill but also surpass the expectations of both users and stakeholders. This chapter ventures into the complex domain of product quality assurance, emphasizing the strategic adoption of automated testing and the development of a comprehensive test automation strategy. Furthermore, we will examine the critical role of architectural tests and outline the roles and responsibilities integral to QA processes.

In this chapter, we will explore the following key areas:

- **The Essence of Automated Testing**: Unpacking the pivotal role automated testing plays in maintaining and enhancing product quality over time.

- **Mastering Unit Testing**: Strategies for crafting unit tests that are meaningful and contribute significantly to software reliability.

- **Rethinking Test Coverage Metrics**: A critical evaluation of test coverage metrics and their real impact on software quality assurance efforts.

A. Souza, *Tech Leadership Playbook*, https://doi.org/10.1007/979-8-8688-0543-1_5

- **Crafting an Effective Test Automation Strategy**: Guidelines for formulating a test automation strategy that aligns with project objectives and team capabilities.

- **Defining Roles and Responsibilities**: Establishing clear roles and responsibilities within the QA process to foster collaboration and accountability.

As we delve into the depths of product quality assurance, we will learn that adapting testing to the rapid pace of Agile iterations necessitates a "shift left" approach. This paradigm shift in the agile development process signifies that testing begins much earlier in the application life cycle. It advocates for the entire team's involvement in delivering high-quality products swiftly and emphasizes continuous improvement while upholding quality and reliability.

Navigating the Balance of Automated Testing

Automated testing is a cornerstone of modern software development, essential for ensuring that our systems remain reliable and effective. It's the safeguard that ensures our systems operate as intended, even as we introduce new features or refactor existing code.

Why Invest in Automated Tests?

The primary motivation behind writing automated tests is to improve confidence. Whenever we change or add something, we want to be sure it doesn't break anything. Automated tests help us do just that, without having to check everything by hand every time.. This confidence is not just for the developers or the product team but extends to stakeholders and, ultimately, the users who rely on the software to perform flawlessly.

The Dilemma of Over-testing

Martin Fowler, a luminary in software development, posits that while testing is indispensable, it's indeed possible to test too much. The litmus test for over-testing, according to Fowler, is if removing certain tests does not diminish the overall confidence in the system's functionality.

Kent Beck, another esteemed figure known for introducing Test-Driven Development (TDD), echoes a similar sentiment. He articulates that the goal isn't to amass unit tests but to test sufficiently to achieve a good level of confidence. He succinctly states, "I get paid for code that works, not for tests," underscoring the philosophy of testing as little as possible to maintain confidence.

Think about getting rid of most of your unit tests. If you consistently need to fix your unit tests with every code refactor, it's worth questioning their utility. Unit tests should give you confidence that changes in your code haven't impacted the desired behavior of your application unit. If they're not serving this purpose and instead require frequent updates, you're only fooling yourself. It might be time to discard them and focus on writing proper tests that truly validate your unit behavior

Optimizing for Confidence, Not Coverage

This introduces a crucial concept: optimizing for confidence rather than quantity. It's about striking a balance, ensuring that each test adds value and enhances confidence without redundantly covering the same ground across unit, module, and end-to-end (E2E) tests. Acknowledging the significant investment in writing and maintaining automated tests, it becomes clear that each test should be purposeful and carefully considered.

The Misconception of Code Coverage

Code coverage, often seen as a metric of testing completeness, can be misleading. High lines of code coverage do not guarantee readiness for real-world scenarios, nor do they ensure the quality or defect-free operation of the system. The fallacy lies in equating code coverage with code quality—a correlation that has been statistically debunked.

The danger of code coverage metrics is their potential to distract from the essence of software development: addressing and fulfilling use cases. For instance, setting arbitrary thresholds, such as not shipping code with coverage below 80%, can lead to the proliferation of trivial tests that add little value or confidence but merely inflate coverage statistics.

However, as Martin Fowler points out, code coverage is not without its merits. It serves as a useful tool for identifying untested code, offering insights into areas that may require attention. The key is to leverage coverage as a guide to uncovering untested paths, not as the sole indicator of quality or completeness.

In summary, by embracing a balanced testing strategy, informed by the wisdom of industry experts, we can navigate the complexities of software development with assurance, focusing on delivering code that works, satisfies user needs, and stands the test of time.

Crafting an Effective Test Strategy for Agile Development

In the fast-paced world of agile software development, the traditional approach to testing often falls short. The iterative nature of agile requires a more dynamic and integrated testing methodology, commonly referred to as the "shift left" approach. This strategy emphasizes the importance of integrating testing early and throughout the software development life cycle, fundamentally changing how teams approach quality assurance (QA).

The Shift Left Approach: Early and Continuous Testing

The "shift left" concept in agile development signifies a fundamental shift in the testing paradigm. By moving testing activities earlier in the development life cycle, we ensure that quality is built into the product from the start. This approach requires developers to take ownership of QA, which entails writing, executing, and maintaining tests for the code they produce. This direct involvement encourages the entire team to take part in delivering high-quality products rapidly and efficiently to the customer.

Who Writes the Tests?

With the shift left approach, the responsibility for creating and managing tests falls predominantly on the developers. This responsibility ensures that testing is not an afterthought but an integral part of the development process from the very beginning. Engaging developers in the testing process fosters a culture of quality and accountability, ensuring that everyone on the team is committed to the product's overall excellence.

QA engineers play a vital role in solidifying the testing strategy, helping reviewing tests, and crafting end-to-end (E2E) tests that encapsulate the user journey in terms comprehensible to the business. Developers and QA engineers now collaborate more closely than ever for the quality of the software. However, gone are the days when developers simply handed off the responsibility for testing their code to testers. In the following section, we will delve deeper into the shared responsibilities of the team.

131

A Progressive Test Strategy

An effective test strategy in agile development begins with the smallest testable components and gradually expands to include larger parts of the system (Figure 5-1). This incremental approach ensures thorough coverage and facilitates early detection of issues.

- **Unit Testing**: The foundation of the testing pyramid, unit testing, focuses on verifying the functionality of individual components in isolation. The goal is to ensure that each component behaves as expected. It's important to note that the "unit" in this context refers to the smallest testable part of the application, which could be a package rather than just a single class.

- **Module Testing**: Once unit testing has validated the behavior of individual components, module testing examines how these components work together. This phase tests the interaction between units, identifying any issues that arise from their integration. Module testing is crucial for ensuring that the software's architecture is sound and that components integrate seamlessly.

- **UI Testing**: User Interface (UI) testing is essential for ensuring that the application functions correctly. UI tests validate the interactive aspects of the application, ensuring that users can interact with the software as intended.

- **End-to-End (E2E) Testing**: The culmination of the testing strategy, E2E testing, evaluates the system's functionality from the user's perspective. It involves testing the integrated system to verify that various user flows work as intended. E2E tests simulate real user scenarios, such as logging in, making transactions, or viewing account balances, to ensure that the system meets the users' needs and expectations.

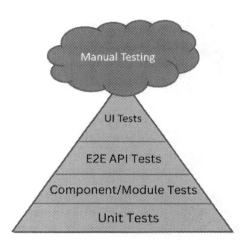

Figure 5-1. *Test pyramid*

Redefining Unit Testing

The concept of unit testing has evolved significantly since its inception. Initially, many developers interpreted unit testing as the need to create a direct test for every public method of every class. However, this approach has led to a common misunderstanding of the core purpose of unit testing, shifting the focus from testing the behavior of the system to testing its implementation.

The Misconception of Unit Testing

The traditional approach to unit testing—targeting every public method with a corresponding test—has inadvertently led to tests that are overly dependent on the specific design of the code. This design dependency means that any refactoring or evolution of the codebase necessitates a parallel overhaul of the tests, which can be both time-consuming and error prone.

What confidence would you have refactoring a code that requires rewrite of the tests? Instead of aiding the development process by providing confidence in the code's functionality, this method of testing often becomes a burden, complicating refactoring efforts and providing little assurance of continued correct behavior.

Avoiding Mock Hell

In pursuit of exhaustive unit testing, developers can find themselves entangled in "mock hell," where the complexity and maintenance overhead of mocks and stubs outweigh their benefits. This over-reliance on mocks not only obscures the intent of the tests but also creates brittle test suites that hinder rather than help refactoring efforts.

Embracing a New Definition of Unit Testing

To harness the true power of unit testing, it's essential to break free from the narrow definition that ties tests to specific methods and implementations. Instead, unit testing should be reconceived as a tool for verifying the behavior of components within the system. By focusing on components—such as user, product, or order modules—and their public interfaces, developers can create tests that are more resilient to changes in the underlying code structure.

This behavior-driven approach to unit testing emphasizes the functionality and outcomes that matter to the end user, rather than the internal workings of individual methods (Figure 5-2). It involves writing tests that cover the expected behaviors of each component, ensuring that all aspects of its functionality are correctly implemented and remain so through subsequent changes and refactoring.

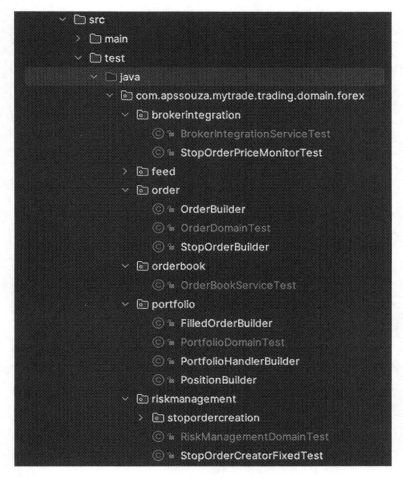

Figure 5-2. *Behavior-driven unit tests*

Implementing Behavior-Driven Unit Tests

To effectively implement behavior-driven unit tests, consider the following strategies:

- **Focus on the Public Interface**: Concentrate your testing efforts on the interactions that external entities have with the component, rather than its internal implementation details.

- **Define Clear Behavior Scenarios**: Identify and document the key behaviors that each component should exhibit, using these scenarios as the basis for your tests.

- **Use Mocks carefully**: While mocks can be valuable for isolating the component under test, avoid overusing them. Aim for a balance that allows you to verify behavior without creating a tangled web of dependencies.

In summary, by shifting the focus of unit testing from rigid method-based tests to flexible behavior-driven tests, developers can create more durable, useful, and maintainable test suites. This approach not only facilitates easier refactoring and code evolution but also ensures that the tests continue to provide meaningful feedback about the system's functionality. Freeing yourself from the outdated definition of unit testing and embracing a behavior-focused perspective is the key to writing effective unit tests that truly enhance the development process.

Module Testing: Ensuring Cohesive Component Interaction

Module testing, or integration testing, is an essential phase in the software development life cycle where individual components are combined and tested as a group. This testing phase is critical for verifying the functionality of components when they interact with each other, building on the foundation laid by unit testing.

Module Testing Approach

- **Testing from the Public Entry Point**: Module tests should begin at the public entry points of a module, encompassing all the integration points where modules interact. This approach ensures that the module can handle expected and unexpected interactions that mimic real-world usage.

- **Behavioral Coverage**: The focus of module testing should be on the behavior and output of the module as a whole. Tests need to validate that the module performs as expected under various conditions, covering all functional requirements and handling of edge cases.

- **Avoiding Duplication**: Module testing should not replicate the granularity of unit tests but rather focus on the interactions and interfaces between components. While unit testing assesses the correctness of individual components, module testing should verify the connections and data flows between different domains.

- **Beyond Unit Testing**: Once unit testing has confirmed the functionality of individual components within a module, module testing should assess how these components work together. This includes testing joint functionality and the integration of unit-tested parts to uncover any issues that occur only when parts are combined.

- **Use of BDD Frameworks**: Behavior-Driven Development (BDD) frameworks can significantly enhance the readability and clarity of test scenarios. By using natural language constructs, BDD frameworks, like Cucumber or SpecFlow, allow for writing tests that are easy to understand and maintain, making them particularly useful for describing and testing complex interactions in module testing.

- **Mocking External Services**: To ensure module tests are both reliable and fast, external service calls should be mocked. This approach isolates the module from external dependencies, allowing testers to simulate various scenarios and responses from external systems without the need for actual network calls.

Implementing Effective Module Tests

- **Develop Comprehensive Test Cases**: Create test scenarios that cover all paths through the module, focusing on the interaction between components and with external systems.

- **Leverage Mocking and Stubbing**: Use tools and libraries designed for mocking (such as Mockito or Moq) to simulate external dependencies and internal module interactions that are not under test.

- **Integrate BDD Practices**: Incorporate BDD practices to develop a shared understanding of the module's behavior among developers, testers, and stakeholders, and to foster collaboration.

- **Automate and Iterate**: Automate module tests to run as part of the continuous integration process, ensuring that integration issues are detected and addressed promptly.

Module testing is a critical step that ensures the integrated components of software work together seamlessly and meet the required specifications. By focusing on interactions and leveraging modern testing practices like BDD, developers can create more robust and reliable software. Proper module testing reduces bugs in production by catching integration errors early in the development cycle and plays a crucial role in the overall quality assurance process.

Mastering End-to-End Testing in Software Development

End-to-end (E2E) testing is a critical phase in the software testing life cycle, where entire applications are tested in a scenario that mimics real-world usage to ensure all integrated components function together as expected. Unlike other testing methodologies that may focus on specific sections or layers of an application, E2E testing evaluates the system's overall health, functionality, and its interactions with external systems and infrastructure.

Why Focus on API Layer for E2E Testing?

E2E testing is often perceived as challenging and resource-intensive, primarily due to the complexities involved in testing through the user interface (UI). To mitigate these challenges, conducting E2E tests at the API layer is highly advantageous:

- **Speed and Efficiency**: API tests are generally faster and less prone to errors compared to UI tests, which are slower and more susceptible to minor changes in the UI.

- **Cost-effectiveness**: Since API tests require less maintenance and can be executed more rapidly, they reduce the overall cost of testing.

- **Broader Test Coverage**: APIs power the core functionalities and data transactions within applications, thus testing at this layer ensures that the system operates correctly under various scenarios without the overhead of automating the UI.

E2E test plans should mimic actual user behaviors to validate the entire application flow. Examples of user-level stories might include:

- "A user can log in."

- "A user can make a deposit."

- "A user can view their balance."

These stories guide the creation of test scenarios that ensure the application performs intended functions in real-world conditions.

To maximize the effectiveness of E2E testing:

- **Automated Triggers**: E2E tests should be automated and triggered by any significant change or deployment in intermediary services. This helps in continuously validating the workflow and catching regressions early.

- **Continuous Integration (CI)**: Integrating E2E tests into the CI pipeline ensures that every change is validated, maintaining the stability and reliability of the application.

Characteristics of Robust E2E Tests

- **Black Box Nature**: E2E tests should be designed as black box tests where the internal structure of the application is not considered. This approach simulates an external user's interaction with the application.

- **Resilience**: Tests need to be resilient and not be influenced by existing data or parallel executions. This may involve setting up isolated test environments or data setups that mimic fresh installations of the application.

- **Infrastructure and Configuration Testing**: Beyond functional testing, E2E tests should also validate the application's infrastructure and configuration settings to ensure the deployment environment itself does not introduce errors.

- **QA Engineer Ownership**: E2E tests should ideally be owned and maintained by QA engineers who specialize in understanding application complexities and user requirements. This ownership ensures that tests remain focused, up-to-date, and aligned with the software's end-user needs.

End-to-end testing serves as a comprehensive method for verifying the integrated performance and reliability of entire software applications. By focusing E2E testing on the API layer, leveraging automated triggers, and ensuring test resilience, organizations can achieve higher confidence in their software deployments. As a crucial part of regression testing, E2E helps secure a seamless user experience, ultimately supporting the delivery of high-quality software products.

UI Tests: Balancing Coverage and Cost in Software Quality Assurance

In the quest for creating a resilient and user-friendly application, UI testing stands as a critical component of the software testing strategy. It ensures that users experience the application as intended and that the interface responds correctly to user interactions. However, an effective UI testing strategy is not just about coverage; it's about smart investment in the types of tests that provide the best return on investment. This section explores the strategic approach to UI testing, emphasizing integration testing and judicious use of end-to-end (E2E) tests.

Prioritizing Integration Over Unit Testing

While unit tests serve as the bedrock of a stable codebase, investing more heavily in integration tests can often yield greater dividends. Integration tests offer insights into how well different parts of the application work together, providing a closer approximation of real-world usage. For a robust testing suite, the focus should shift toward these integration tests, which effectively capture the interactions within the application.

The Cost of E2E UI Testing

E2E UI testing, particularly with tools like Cypress, is invaluable for verifying critical user journeys. However, these tests can be costly to run and maintain due to their complexity and the overhead involved in simulating the full range of user interactions. Given this, it's prudent to reserve E2E UI tests for the most critical areas of your application—those user paths that are essential for the operation and revenue generation, such as checkout flows in an e-commerce app.

Embracing Jest for Integration Testing

For integration tests, Jest emerges as an efficient and effective tool, particularly within the JavaScript and React ecosystems. Jest is well-suited for testing the interactions between components, verifying that they coalesce seamlessly to form a cohesive user experience.

Integration Testing in Action

Integration testing covers the collective behavior of various components. In the context of a React application, where components range from simple to complex and are interdependent, integration testing verifies their combined functionality. It is important to note that the backend is not included in the integration tests, and therefore should be mocked.

Take, for instance, a to-do list application. Integration tests play a vital role in ensuring that components such as ListItem, ListItemAction, ListGroup, and TodoListView perform harmoniously. These tests would cover scenarios like adding a new task, marking a task as complete, editing an existing item, or removing it—simulating the user's perspective and actions.

In conclusion, the strategy of prioritizing integration testing over unit testing, while selectively applying E2E UI tests, aligns the development process with the ultimate goal of delivering a quality user experience. By utilizing tools like Jest for integration testing, and reserving tools like Cypress for the most critical paths, teams can maintain an effective balance between test coverage, execution cost, and overhead maintenance.

Quality Assurance Roles and Responsibilities

To ensure the delivery of high-quality software in an agile and secure way, it's essential to clearly define the roles and responsibilities within the development team. In the following, we outline the key responsibilities for QA engineers, developers, team leads, and product owners.

QA Engineer

- **Wear the User Hat**: Emphasize issues or poor experiences from the user's perspective.

- **Review User-facing Documentation**: Ensure that all public documentation accurately reflects the product's usage and features.

- **Test Acceptance Criteria**: Manually verify that all acceptance criteria are met.

- **Clarify Test Steps**: Ensure that tickets describe the steps needed to test the feature or fix.

- **Provide Test Evidence**: Attach evidence of testing to the corresponding ticket.

- **Sign off on User Story Releases**: Approve user stories for release after thorough testing.

- **Review Module Tests**: Examine tests for individual components for completeness and accuracy.

- **Implement Automated E2E Tests**: Create automated tests that cover the entire user journey.

- **Maintain E2E Test Suite**: Regularly check that E2E tests are passing and up-to-date.

- **Refine Stories**: Assist in story refinement with a focus on testability and coverage.

Developer

- **Write Unit and Module Tests**: Ensure that code is covered by reliable and comprehensive tests.

- **Review E2E Tests**: Participate in the review process for end-to-end tests.

- **Provide Testing Instructions**: Offer clear guidance for QA engineers on validating user story implementations.

- **Document Complex Solutions**: Create concise documentation for aspects of the code that aren't self-explanatory.

- **Test Tech Tasks**: Take responsibility for testing technical tasks and features.

- **Manage Tech Tasks**: Oversee the completion and closure of technical tasks.

- **Test in Development Environment**: Verify all changes in the development environment before staging.

- **Prepare for Staging**: Release features to the staging environment for final QA checks.

- **Facilitate Quick Sign Off**: Work efficiently to obtain QA engineer signoff for production releases of User stories.

- **Release to Production**: Manage the release process to the production environment.

Team Lead

- **Conduct Code Reviews**: Oversee code reviews to maintain quality and adherence to best practices.

- **Maintain Best Practices**: Document and enforce best coding and testing practices within the team.

- **Breakdown User Stories**: Help divide larger user stories into manageable, deliverable pieces.

- **Review Sprint Deliverables**: Evaluate the completeness and quality of sprint outcomes.

Product Owner

- **Validate User Story Implementation**: Confirm that the development work accurately fulfills the defined user stories.

- **Authorize Story Closure**: Approve the completion of user stories, confirming that all criteria are met.

Conclusion

In this chapter, we have explored various facets of quality assurance in software development, each contributing significantly to the overarching goal of delivering high-quality, reliable software. From redefining automated testing strategies to debunking common misconceptions about code coverage, our journey through this chapter has provided a comprehensive guide on how to strategically approach quality assurance in a dynamic development environment.

Key Takeaways

- **Balancing Automated Testing**: Automation is invaluable, yet it requires strategic thinking. It's crucial to navigate the balance between over-testing and under-testing. Optimizing automated tests for confidence rather than mere coverage ensures that testing efforts add value, are cost-effective, and significantly boost the confidence in the product's reliability without redundancy.

- **Rethinking Code Coverage**: While code coverage is a useful metric, it should not be the sole measure of testing effectiveness. High code coverage does not necessarily equate to high code quality. Focus instead on crafting tests that challenge the system's behavior in real-world scenarios, ensuring readiness and robustness beyond theoretical completeness.

- **Evolving Unit Testing**: The evolution of unit testing from a granular check of every public method to a more behavior-driven approach highlights a shift toward efficiency and relevance in test case creation. This shift helps maintain the focus on what truly matters—ensuring the software behaves as expected under various conditions.

- **Integration in Module Testing**: Module testing, or integration testing, plays a pivotal role by verifying the interaction and integration of individual components. This phase is vital for catching issues that unit tests might miss, ensuring that the components function together seamlessly as intended.

- **Cost-Effective UI and E2E Testing**: Strategically balancing the extent and depth of UI and end-to-end tests is essential. Focusing on the API layer for E2E testing, for example, can provide a high impact at a lower cost compared to exhaustive UI testing, aligning expenditure with outcomes.

- **Clarity in QA Roles**: Defining clear roles and responsibilities within the QA process is crucial for effective teamwork and accountability. Each role, from QA engineers to product owners, must understand their specific duties in ensuring software quality, fostering a collaborative and thorough QA process.

Quality assurance is not just a phase or a set of tasks—it is an integral part of the software development life cycle that demands careful planning, execution, and continuous improvement. By adopting a thoughtful approach to testing, focusing on meaningful coverage, and fostering a culture that values quality, teams can deliver software products that are not only functional but also robust and user-centric. Let this chapter serve as a blueprint for building a strong foundation in quality assurance practices that are adaptable, efficient, and effective.

CHAPTER 6

Software Development Life Cycle (SDLC)

In the rapidly evolving landscape of software development, the Software Development Life Cycle (SDLC) stands as a cornerstone for delivering high-quality software projects. This chapter embarks on a comprehensive journey through the intricacies of the SDLC, revealing its dynamic and adaptable nature that caters to the unique demands of each project, team, and organization.

Understanding the SDLC is not merely about grasping a series of technical steps; it's about appreciating the strategic framework that guides a project from its conceptual phase to successful deployment and beyond. As we delve into this chapter, we will explore the critical methodologies, tools, and best practices that underpin effective software development.

One of the core themes we will examine is the flexibility in source control strategies, highlighting the evolution from traditional Git Flow to the more agile Trunk-Based Development. This comparison underscores the importance of selecting the right approach to meet the agility and efficiency demands of modern software projects.

We will also navigate the essential roles of Continuous Integration, Continuous Delivery, and Continuous Deployment within a DevOps culture. By understanding these processes, you'll see how they contribute to a seamless workflow that balances automation with rigorous quality assurance.

© The Editor(s) (if applicable) and The Author(s),
under exclusive license to APress Media, LLC, part of Springer Nature 2024
A. Souza, *Tech Leadership Playbook*, https://doi.org/10.1007/979-8-8688-0543-1_6

The importance of robust testing environments cannot be overstated, and this chapter will shed light on why mimicking production conditions is crucial for early issue detection. By the time software reaches the staging environment, it should be a refined product ready for the final step to production.

Our exploration of CI/CD pipeline architecture will provide you with detailed insights into building, testing, and deploying software in a systematic, reliable manner. This structured approach is key to managing the complexities of modern development projects, ensuring consistent delivery of new features to users.

Prepare to dive deep into the SDLC, understanding its foundational concepts, strategic importance, and practical applications. By the end of this chapter, you will be well-versed in how to leverage the SDLC to deliver software excellence, ensuring your projects are both efficient and impactful.

Git Flow vs. Trunk-Based Development

In the realm of software development, choosing the right version control workflow is pivotal for facilitating efficient collaboration and enabling continuous deployment. Two prominent strategies have emerged: Git Flow and Trunk-Based Development. Each offers distinct advantages and caters to different project needs, but recent trends and the push toward more agile practices have seen a shift in preference.

Understanding Git Flow

Git Flow (Figure 6-1) is a branching model designed for projects that benefit from a structured release cycle. It involves multiple branches for different purposes—features, releases, hotfixes, and development—merging back into the main branch at designated stages. This model provides a clear pathway for new features and fixes, ensuring stability for each release.

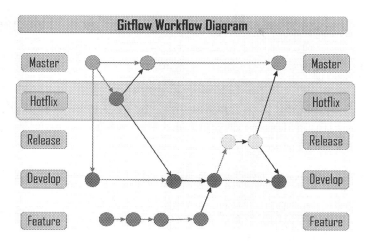

Figure 6-1. *Gitflow workflow diagram*

However, Git Flow introduces complexity that can be counterproductive for teams aiming for continuous deployment. The multiple branches necessitate significant management and can slow down the integration process, making it less ideal for environments where speed and flexibility are paramount.

Why Git Flow May Fall Short

In modern development practices, where the goal is to deploy small increments of change rapidly to production, Git Flow's structured approach can become a bottleneck. The separation between development and deployment phases can hinder the flow of updates, leading to delays and a backlog of features waiting to be released.

Advocating for Trunk-Based Development

Trunk-based development (Figure 6-2) is a software development strategy that emphasizes simplicity and agility in managing code changes. It encourages developers to work in short-lived branches and merge

153

changes back to the main branch frequently—often daily. This approach minimizes code divergence from the main codebase, enhances continuous integration practices, and paves the way for more efficient continuous deployment.

Trunk-based development is characterized by a few key practices that promote rapid integration of changes and high collaboration among team members. Here's a step-by-step explanation of the process:

- **Creating a Short-Lived Branch**: Developers start by creating a new branch from the main branch (commonly referred to as the trunk). The key characteristic of this branch is its short lifespan, typically not more than a day or two. This practice ensures that changes are small and manageable, which simplifies merging and reduces the risk of conflicts.

- **Making Commits**: Once the branch is created, developers make changes by adding commits to this short-lived branch. These changes should be focused and relevant to a specific task or feature to maintain clarity and manageability. Keeping the commits small and frequent within the branch helps in tracking changes and understanding the history of developments.

- **Opening a Pull Request**: After the necessary changes have been committed, the next step is to integrate these changes back into the main branch. This is typically done through a pull request (or merge request), which serves as a platform for code review. During this phase, other team members review the changes, discuss potential improvements, and finally approve the merge if everything is in order.

- **Merging and Tagging**: Once the pull request is approved, the changes are merged into the main branch. Immediately following the merge, a new tag is created for the merged commit. This tagging helps in marking significant points in the repository's history, like the completion of features, fixes, or releases. Tags play a crucial role in identifying the versions of code that are to be deployed.

- **Triggering Deployment**: The final step in the trunk-based development process is the deployment. The creation of a new tag can trigger an automated deployment process, which deploys the latest changes to production or staging environments. This step is crucial for continuous deployment, allowing teams to quickly and frequently deliver improvements and new features to users.

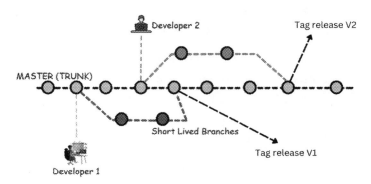

Figure 6-2. *Trunk-based workflow diagram*

The Advantages of Trunk-Based Development

Trunk-Based Development aligns more closely with the principles of Agile and DevOps by emphasizing quick, iterative updates and promoting a culture of continuous improvement. This approach reduces the complexity associated with managing multiple branches, enabling teams to respond more swiftly to changes and deploy updates faster. By keeping the development process streamlined and focused on the trunk, teams can ensure that every commit is potentially releasable, significantly enhancing deployment frequency and product quality.

- **Minimized Code Divergence**: By merging changes back to the main branch frequently, the code divergence is minimized, reducing the complexity and risk associated with merging larger, more infrequent updates.

- **Enhanced Collaboration**: With all developers working closely with the trunk, collaboration is enhanced, and integration issues are identified and resolved promptly.

- **Faster Release Cycles**: Frequent merging facilitates faster and more reliable release cycles, aligning with agile principles of rapid iteration and feedback.

- **Improved Feedback Loop**: Continuous integration and deployment facilitate a faster feedback loop with users, allowing teams to adapt and improve the product rapidly

While Git Flow offers a structured approach suitable for projects with defined release schedules, Trunk-Based Development stands out as the superior strategy for teams prioritizing continuous deployment and agility.

Continuous Integration vs. Continuous Delivery vs. Continuous Deployment

In the evolving landscape of software development, the concepts of Continuous Integration (CI), Continuous Delivery, and Continuous (Figure 6-3) Deployment represent crucial methodologies aimed at improving the efficiency and reliability of producing and releasing high-quality software.

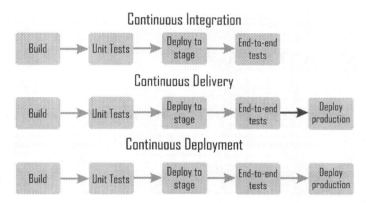

Figure 6-3. *Different CI/CD workflow diagram*

Continuous Integration (CI)

Continuous Integration (CI) is a development practice where developers frequently integrate their code changes into a shared repository, preferably multiple times a day. Each integration is automatically verified by building the project and running automated tests. This approach aims to identify and resolve integration errors quickly, maintain a high quality of code, and reduce the time it takes to validate and release new software updates.

Continuous Delivery

Building on the foundation of CI, Continuous Delivery extends the automated pipeline to include the automatic release of code to a staging environment after the build and test stages. It ensures that the codebase is always in a deployable state, enabling teams to release new changes to customers quickly and safely at the push of a button. Continuous Delivery automates the delivery process but stops short of automating the final step of moving to production, which remains a manual decision.

Continuous Deployment

Continuous Deployment takes Continuous Delivery one step further by automating the release of every successful build to the production environment. This means that every change that passes all stages of your production pipeline is released to your customers with no human intervention, and only a failed test will prevent a new change to be deployed to production.

Advocating for Continuous Delivery

While each of these methodologies plays a critical role in modern software development practices, Continuous Delivery emerges as the recommended approach for most teams. Continuous Delivery strikes a balance between the rigorous validation of CI and the automation of Continuous Deployment. It ensures that software can be released at any moment, providing teams with the flexibility to decide when and how to release to production based on business requirements, not just technical capabilities.

Continuous Delivery offers several advantages that make it the best option for many software development teams:

- **Flexibility in Release Timing**: Teams can choose the most opportune moments for release, aligning software updates with market demands, customer feedback, or strategic business goals.

- **Higher Release Safety**: By automating the delivery process up to but not including the final push to production, teams can conduct final reviews or approval processes, ensuring that every release meets not only technical standards but also business expectations.

- **Improved Product Quality**: Continuous Delivery encourages the use of automated testing and staging environments, which leads to higher product quality and user satisfaction.

Continuous Delivery and Segregation of Duties

One of the essential benefits of Continuous Delivery is its compatibility with the segregation of duties policy, a principle crucial for security and compliance in many organizations. Continuous Delivery allows for clear delineation of responsibilities between writing code, testing, and deploying. This separation ensures that no individual has unilateral control over the entire software development life cycle, significantly reducing the risk of errors or malicious changes making their way into production.

In summary, as software development teams strive to improve their deployment practices, Continuous Delivery offers a robust framework that not only accelerates the pace of releases but also enhances the overall security and quality of the software. By adopting Continuous Delivery, teams can enjoy the benefits of automated pipelines while retaining control over the final release process, ensuring that every deployment aligns with both technical standards and business objectives.

Navigating Multiple Testing Environments: The Path to Reliable Releases

In the journey toward releasing robust and error-free software, multiple testing environments play a critical role. While the configuration and number of these environments can vary based on team requirements and project complexity, three core environments—Development (Dev), Staging, and Production—are commonly employed by most companies. This section explores the purpose of each and how they contribute to a streamlined and efficient release process.

The Trio of Essential Environments

- **Development Environment**: The Dev environment is where the new code first lands and where the first environment where devs test the new feature in an integrated environment. This environment is highly dynamic and subject to frequent changes, making it unsuitable for thorough testing or client reviews.

- **Staging Environment**: Serving as a bridge between development and production, the Staging environment is crucial for conducting final tests in conditions that closely mimic the production environment. The key distinction between Dev and Staging lies in the quality of data and the stability of the environment. Staging is meant to replicate the production setup as closely as possible, using real data clones or data sanitized of sensitive information. This setup provides a reliable platform for comprehensive testing, bug tracking, and performance evaluation without the risks associated with live environments.

- **Production Environment**: The ultimate destination for any software development process, the Production environment, is where the software is accessible to end users. Maintaining the integrity and stability of this environment is paramount, as it directly impacts the user experience and trust in the product.

The Rationale Behind Dev and Staging

The rationale for maintaining separate Dev and Staging environments hinges on the necessity of having a stable, non-production setting for thorough testing. While the Dev environment allows for individual development and initial testing, its often unstable nature and the use of testing data limit its utility for final quality assurance processes. The Staging environment, by contrast, provides a more controlled and accurate testing ground, essential for catching issues that may not be apparent in the Dev environment due to the difference in data quality.

Staging: The Final Checkpoint Before Release

The Staging environment plays a pivotal role as the final checkpoint before a release is approved for production. It is here that Quality Assurance (QA) teams and Product Owners (PO) conduct exhaustive tests to validate functionality, performance, security, and user experience. This environment is instrumental for QA and PO to sign off on a release, ensuring that all aspects of the software meet or exceed the established criteria for quality and reliability.

The collective signoff in the Staging environment is a critical step in the release process, offering one last opportunity to catch and rectify any issues before they affect the end user. This practice not only safeguards the product's integrity but also reinforces the commitment to delivering high-quality software.

Architecting an Efficient CI/CD Pipeline

In the realm of modern software development, the Continuous Integration/Continuous Deployment (CI/CD) pipeline is a cornerstone of delivering high-quality software at a rapid pace. Regardless of the specific tools or programming languages you choose for your pipeline, the structure of your CI/CD process plays a pivotal role in its effectiveness. To maximize efficiency and ensure comprehensive quality checks, your pipeline should include at least four fundamental steps: test, build, deploy, and end-to-end test.

The Four Essential Steps of CI/CD

- **Test**: The first step in any robust CI/CD pipeline involves running automated tests to catch bugs and ensure that the new code integrates seamlessly with the existing codebase. This step typically includes unit tests and module tests, which provide early detection of issues at the lowest levels of the application.

- **Build**: Following successful testing, the next step is to build the application. This process compiles the code into executable or deployable packages, preparing it for deployment in a staging or production environment.

- **Deploy**: Deployment is the process of releasing the newly built version of the application to a staging or production environment. This step is crucial for the practical evaluation of the application in a scenario that closely mimics the end user experience.

- **End-to-End Test**: The final step involves conducting comprehensive end-to-end tests on the deployed application. These tests simulate real user scenarios to ensure that the application functions correctly as a whole and that all integrated components interact as expected.

Essential Jobs Within the CI/CD Pipeline

To ensure that your application meets the highest standards of code quality and security, your CI/CD pipeline should incorporate the following jobs:

- **Unit Test**: Validates the functionality of individual units of code, ensuring they behave as intended in isolation.

- **Module Test**: Tests the interaction between components that comprise the application, identifying issues in the integration of different parts of the system.

- **Checkstyle**: Analyzes the code to ensure it adheres to defined coding standards and conventions, promoting readability and maintainability.

- **Cyclomatic Complexity**: Measures the complexity of the code's structure, helping to identify overly complex methods that may be prone to errors or difficult to maintain.

- **Security Static Analysis**: Scans the code for known security vulnerabilities, ensuring that the application is not exposed to common security threats.

- **Code Linter**: Performs static code analysis to detect potential errors, bugs, stylistic errors, and suspicious constructs, encouraging a cleaner, more error-free codebase.

The core message of this section is clear: setting up a CI/CD pipeline with these four critical steps and incorporating essential jobs such as unit testing, module testing, and various code quality checks ensures a rigorous assessment of your software's functionality, security, and maintainability before it reaches your users. By adhering to these practices, teams can significantly reduce the likelihood of bugs, improve code quality, and accelerate the delivery of new features and updates, all while maintaining high standards of software excellence.

Navigating the Release Life Cycle in Modern Software Development

The Release Life Cycle is a critical component of the software development process, dictating the path from code conception to deployment in the production environment (Figure 6-4). This structured approach ensures that every change introduced to the software is rigorously tested, approved by key stakeholders, and seamlessly integrated into the live application. Let's delve into the life cycle stages that guide a feature from development to production.

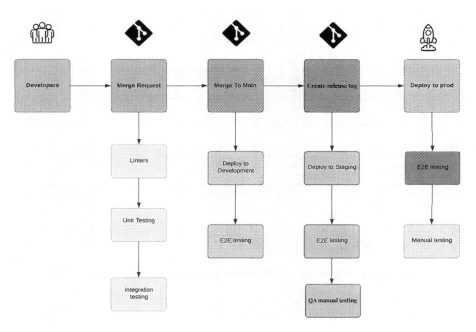

Figure 6-4. *Release cycle diagram*

The Stages of the Release Life Cycle

- **Merging and Deployment to Development**: Initially, developers merge their completed work into the main branch following at least one peer approval. This merged code is automatically deployed to the Development environment, where preliminary end-to-end (E2E) tests are conducted to validate new changes.

- **Staging Deployment and Testing**: Once manual testing and automated E2E tests in the Development environment are satisfactory, developers trigger the deployment to the Staging environment. This environment is crucial for conducting more comprehensive tests that mimic real-world usage without affecting the live product.

- **QA Testing in Staging**: In the Staging environment, QA engineers and Product Owners can undertake manual testing and commence the development of automated E2E tests specific to the new user story. This stage is pivotal for ensuring that all aspects of the new feature function as intended in a controlled setting that closely resembles production.

- **Production Release**: Following successful testing in Staging and obtaining the necessary approvals from QA engineers and the Product Owner, developers proceed to release the feature to the Production environment. This step is performed with great care to ensure that the live user experience remains uninterrupted and enhanced by the new additions.

- **User Story Closure**: Post-deployment, developers officially close the user stories, marking the completion of the feature's development cycle, contingent on the final nod from the Product Owner.

- **Finalizing Automated E2E Tests**: Concurrently, QA finalizes the automated E2E tests covering the full user journey of the newly introduced feature, further bolstering the test suite for future development.

Detailed Release Processes

- **Release to the Development Environment**: Automatic deployment to the Development environment follows each merge to the main branch. This phase is crucial for running automated E2E tests to ensure that the new code integrates seamlessly with the existing codebase.

- **Release to the Staging Environment**: The move to Staging is initiated by creating a release-* tag, signifying the readiness of the code for more rigorous testing. Staging serves as the final rehearsal space before the feature encounters real users.

- **Release to the Production Environment**: The transition of code to the Production environment is a deliberate manual process. Following the green light from Staging E2E tests, a manual trigger enables the deployment to Production, marking the culmination of the Release Life Cycle.

In conclusion, the Release Life Cycle embodies the discipline and structured approach essential for delivering high-quality software in today's fast-paced development environments. By adhering to these stages—each with its distinct focus on testing, approval, and deployment—teams can ensure that new features are not only functionally sound but also aligned with user expectations and business objectives. This life cycle fosters a culture of quality, collaboration, and continuous improvement, essential pillars for achieving excellence in software development.

Conclusion

As we reach the end of our journey through the Software Development Life Cycle (SDLC), it's evident that mastering SDLC is crucial for the successful delivery of software projects. This chapter has unpacked the complexities and nuances of the SDLC, revealing it as a dynamic and adaptable framework tailored to meet the specific needs of each project, team, and organization.

Key Takeaways

- **Flexibility in Methodologies**: The comparison between Git Flow and Trunk-Based Development illustrates the evolution of source control strategies to accommodate the increasing demand for agility in software projects. While Git Flow offers a highly structured approach suitable for certain development environments, Trunk-Based Development aligns better with practices geared toward rapid integration and continuous delivery.

- **Embracing CI/CD**: We explored the critical roles of Continuous Integration, Continuous Delivery, and Continuous Deployment within a DevOps culture. The adaptability of Continuous Delivery emerged as particularly significant, striking an optimal balance between the need for automated workflows and the necessity for quality assurance in software releases.

- **Importance of Testing Environments**: The discussion on multiple testing environments underscored the importance of mimicking production conditions to detect issues early. This practice ensures that by the time software reaches the staging environment, it is polished and primed for a successful production deployment.

- **CI/CD Pipeline Architecture**: Detailed insights into the architecture of CI/CD pipelines highlighted the structured, systematic approach required to effectively build, test, and deploy software. This structure is vital for managing the complexities of modern software development and ensuring consistent and reliable feature delivery to users.

- **People and Principles Over Processes and Tools**: Lastly, the SDLC is not just about the processes and tools but also about the people involved and the principles that guide them. It is a cycle of continuous learning and improvement, where commitment to best practices, adaptability, and a relentless focus on value delivery are paramount.

The Software Development Life Cycle is a foundational concept that spans beyond mere technical executions to encompass strategic planning and thoughtful execution. As software development continues to evolve, so too should our approach to managing the life cycle of our projects. By embracing both the structured and adaptive aspects of SDLC, teams are better positioned to navigate the challenges of modern development environments and drive successful outcomes. Whether it is through selecting the most suitable development approach, optimizing CI/CD processes, or ensuring robust testing environments, the SDLC remains at the heart of delivering software excellence.

CHAPTER 7

Observability and Monitoring

In the complex and dynamic world of software development, the ability to monitor and understand the internal state of systems in production has never been more crucial. This need gives rise to the concept of Observability, a term that has quickly become central to discussions on software reliability, performance, and security. Observability goes beyond traditional monitoring, offering a more nuanced and comprehensive view of what's happening within our applications. This chapter delves into the essence of observability, its foundational pillars, and its profound impact on enhancing security within software systems.

Observability is the measure of how well internal states of a system can be inferred from knowledge of its external outputs. It's a property of systems that allows developers and operations teams to diagnose and understand the behavior of their software in production. With observability, teams can quickly identify issues, understand their impact, and take corrective action, often before users are even aware of a problem. This proactive approach to system management is vital in today's fast-paced, always-on digital environment.

© The Editor(s) (if applicable) and The Author(s),
under exclusive license to APress Media, LLC, part of Springer Nature 2024
A. Souza, *Tech Leadership Playbook*, https://doi.org/10.1007/979-8-8688-0543-1_7

The Three Pillars of Observability

Central to the concept of observability are the three pillars: logs, metrics, and traces (Figure 7-1). Each plays a unique role in providing insight into the application and its performance:

- **Logs**: Text records of events that have occurred within the application. Logs are invaluable for understanding the sequence of actions leading up to an event or issue, offering a detailed narrative of the system's behavior over time.

- **Metrics**: Aggregated numerical data that represent the measurements of various aspects of the system's performance and health. Metrics provide a high-level overview of system state, making it easier to spot trends and anomalies over time.

- **Traces**: Detailed descriptions of individual requests or transactions as they move through various services and processes within an application. Traces allow teams to follow the path of a request, pinpointing where delays or errors occur in the system's workflow.

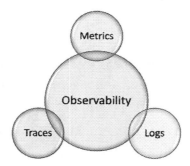

Figure 7-1. *The three pillars of observability*

How Does Observability Work?

Observability platforms work by continuously identifying and gathering performance telemetry through the integration of existing instrumentation embedded within application and infrastructure components. These platforms also offer tools to add additional instrumentation where needed.

Typically, an observability platform collects metrics, traces, and logs and connects them in real time. This integrated approach provides DevOps teams, site reliability engineering (SRE) teams, and IT personnel with thorough contextual information about what is happening, where it is happening, and why it is happening. This comprehensive view is crucial for diagnosing and addressing application performance issues effectively.

Why is Observability Important?

Thanks to Observability, cross-functional teams who work on highly distributed systems, especially in an enterprise environment, can react more quickly and effectively to precise queries.

One can identify what's slowing down the application's performance and work toward fixing it before it impacts the overall performance or leads to downtime.

The **benefits of Observability** extend beyond IT use cases. When you gather and examine observability data, you have a window into the effects your digital services are having on your organization. This access allows you to monitor the results of your user experience SLOs, check that software releases fulfill business goals, and prioritize business choices based on what matters most.

Observability vs. Monitoring: Understanding the Distinction

In the realm of software development and operations, the terms "observability" and "monitoring" are often used interchangeably. However, understanding the nuanced differences between these concepts is crucial for effectively managing system performance and health. This section delves into the definitions of observability and monitoring, highlighting their unique characteristics and how they complement each other in a comprehensive system management strategy.

Monitoring: The Watchful Eye

Monitoring refers to the process of collecting, analyzing, and displaying real-time data about a system's operation. It's about being on the lookout for predefined conditions or thresholds and alerting when those conditions are met or exceeded. Monitoring tools are designed to track the health, performance, and availability of systems, providing teams with vital information on system metrics like CPU usage, memory consumption, and response times. The primary goal of monitoring is to ensure that the system remains within operational parameters and to alert personnel to potential issues before they impact users or business operations.

- **Focused on Knowns**: Monitoring is inherently focused on known quantities—specific metrics and logs that have been identified in advance as indicators of system health.

- **Reactive Nature**: Traditional monitoring is reactive, designed to alert based on predefined conditions. It assumes that you know what could go wrong and that you're watching for those specific conditions.

Observability: Gaining Insight into the Unknown

Observability, while related to monitoring, extends beyond it to offer a more holistic view of system health and behavior. It is the property of a system that allows teams to diagnose and understand issues they didn't anticipate beforehand. Observability encompasses the collection and analysis of logs, metrics, and traces—the three pillars that provide deep insights into the system's internal state. Unlike monitoring, which is about tracking known problems, observability is about exploring the unknown, enabling teams to ask arbitrary questions about their systems without having prior knowledge of what might go wrong.

- **Focused on Unknowns**: Observability is designed to help teams navigate and understand the unknown aspects of their systems. It enables the discovery of issues that were not anticipated during the monitoring setup phase.

- **Proactive Exploration**: With observability, the approach is more proactive. It's about analyzing and understanding system behavior, which allows for more informed decision-making and problem-solving in dynamic, complex environments.

While monitoring is indispensable for day-to-day operations, observability complements it by providing the tools and capabilities needed to understand and solve unforeseen problems. Observability offers a way to ask questions about your system data, thereby uncovering insights that monitoring alone might not reveal. This comprehensive approach enables teams to not only detect and react to known issues but also to explore and understand new or unexpected behaviors within their systems.

Elevating Observability Through Strategic Logging

Logs form the cornerstone of observability, providing a chronological record of events, operations, and errors within an application. Effective logging practices are not just beneficial; they are critical for diagnosing issues, understanding system behavior, and ensuring operational transparency. This section delves into guiding principles and best practices to help teams generate insightful, actionable logs that enhance system observability.

Understanding Log Levels

A well-structured logging strategy categorizes log messages according to their severity and purpose. Adopting the correct log level for each event helps in filtering and analyzing log data, especially during issue diagnosis:

- **DEBUG**: Utilized primarily for detailed system analysis during development or troubleshooting.

- **INFO**: Captures the normal operations of the system, documenting key events and processes.

- **WARN**: Indicates a problem that doesn't directly impact system operation, but may require attention.

- **ERROR**: Marks issues that affect system functionality, potentially impacting the user experience.

- **FATAL**: Used sparingly for critical problems leading to system failure or termination.

Best Practices for Effective Logging

- **Safeguard Sensitive Information**: Always exclude sensitive data like passwords, credit card numbers, and personal identifiers from logs to maintain privacy and compliance.

- **Comprehensive Error Logging**: On encountering an error, log all relevant information needed to reproduce the issue, ensuring efficient troubleshooting.

- **External Service Interactions**: In case of errors with external services, log both the request and response (excluding personally identifiable information (PII)) to aid in debugging.

- **Use of Log Levels**: Log service interactions and failures with appropriate detail, using DEBUG for request-response logging and INFO for service requests. Log bad requests as WARNINGS and always include stack traces and thread names for exceptions in multithreaded applications.

- **Timestamp and Time Zone**: Ensure logs have millisecond resolution timestamps in UTC format to accurately trace events across distributed systems.

- **Log Format and Correlation**: Adopt JSON format for structured logging, facilitating easier parsing and analysis. Use trace IDs and span IDs for log correlation in distributed environments, enabling a cohesive view of transactions or workflows.

- **Logging Environment and Configuration**: At startup, log vital environment configurations such as service URLs and server ports, providing a snapshot of the operational context.

- **Error Handling Philosophy**: Adhere to the principle that an error should be logged or propagated but not both, to avoid duplicate handling and ensure errors are addressed at the correct system layer.

Audit Logging Best Practices

In addition to operational logging, audit logs play a crucial role in security and compliance, tracking critical events such as:

- Input and output validation failures.

- Authentication and authorization attempts.

- Session management issues.

- System errors, connectivity problems, and configuration changes.

- Use of higher-risk functionalities and significant system events like startup or shutdown.

Audit logs should meticulously document these events to support security analysis and regulatory compliance efforts.

Implementing a robust logging strategy is paramount for maintaining high observability within software systems. By adhering to established log levels, safeguarding sensitive information, and ensuring detailed and structured log output, teams can greatly enhance their ability to monitor, diagnose, and optimize their applications. Strategic logging practices not only illuminate the inner workings of complex systems but also fortify security measures and compliance posture, making them indispensable in modern software development and operations.

Centralized Log Management

In the modern landscape of software development and operations, logs are a fundamental part of understanding system behavior and diagnosing issues. However, as systems grow in complexity and scale, managing logs from multiple sources becomes a significant challenge. This is where centralized log management comes into play (Figure 7-2). By aggregating logs from various components into a single, unified system, teams can more effectively monitor, analyze, and act upon their log data. This section explores the importance of centralized log management and how it enhances the efficiency and effectiveness of maintaining complex systems.

Why Centralized Log Management is Essential

- **Unified View of System Activity**: Centralized log management consolidates logs from different sources—applications, servers, databases, and network devices—into a single platform. This unified view allows teams to see the complete picture of system activity, making it easier to correlate events and understand the context of issues.

- **Enhanced Troubleshooting and Incident Response**: When an issue arises, having all logs in one place significantly speeds up the troubleshooting process. Teams can quickly search and filter logs to identify the root cause of problems, reducing the time it takes to resolve incidents and minimizing downtime.

- **Improved Security and Compliance**: Centralized log management plays a critical role in security monitoring and compliance. By aggregating logs, security teams can more effectively detect suspicious activities, investigate security incidents, and ensure compliance with regulatory requirements through comprehensive audit trails.

- **Scalability and Performance**: Managing logs centrally allows for scalable storage and processing capabilities. This ensures that as the volume of log data grows, the system can handle the increased load without degradation in performance. Centralized systems often come with built-in tools for managing large datasets efficiently.

- **Automated Alerting and Monitoring**: Centralized log management systems can integrate with monitoring tools to provide real-time alerts based on specific log patterns or thresholds. This proactive approach allows teams to address potential issues before they escalate, maintaining system reliability and performance.

- **Historical Data and Trend Analysis**: Centralized log management facilitates the storage of historical log data, enabling trend analysis and long-term monitoring. Teams can analyze past logs to identify recurring issues, understand system behavior over time, and make informed decisions about future improvements.

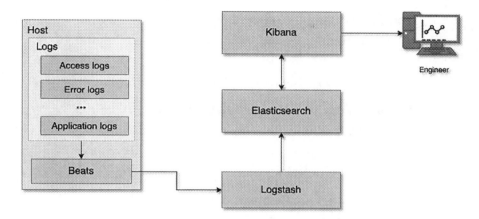

Figure 7-2. *Log processing and analysis using ELK stack*

Implementing Centralized Log Management

To implement centralized log management effectively, consider the following best practices:

- **Choose the Right Tools**: Select a centralized logging solution that fits your needs, such as ELK Stack (Elasticsearch, Logstash, Kibana), Splunk, or Graylog. Ensure it integrates well with your existing systems and can handle the volume and type of log data you generate.

- **Standardize Log Formats**: Implement consistent logging formats across all systems and applications to ensure logs are easily parsed and analyzed. Standardized log formats improve the efficiency of log ingestion and processing.

- **Set Up Structured Logging**: Use structured logging to format log entries in a consistent, machine-readable way (e.g., JSON). Structured logs enable more precise searching, filtering, and analysis.

- **Define Retention Policies**: Establish retention policies to manage the life cycle of log data. Determine how long different types of logs should be retained based on compliance requirements and storage capacity.

- **Implement Access Controls**: Ensure that only authorized personnel have access to log data by implementing robust access control mechanisms. This enhances security and protects sensitive information.

Centralized log management is a cornerstone of effective system monitoring and maintenance. By providing a unified view of system activity, enhancing troubleshooting capabilities, improving security, and enabling scalable log processing, centralized log management ensures that teams can manage their systems more efficiently and respond to issues more rapidly. As systems become increasingly complex, the value of centralized log management in maintaining operational excellence cannot be overstated.

Embracing OpenTelemetry: The Unified Observability Framework

In the quest for comprehensive system observability, developers and operations teams require tools that can seamlessly collect, analyze, and act upon the vast amounts of data generated by modern software applications.

Enter OpenTelemetry, an open source observability framework designed to provide standardized and efficient ways to gather telemetry data for cloud-native software. This section delves into the essence of OpenTelemetry, its components, and its significance in enabling effective observability practices.

The Genesis of OpenTelemetry

OpenTelemetry emerged from the convergence of two prominent observability projects: OpenTracing and OpenCensus. Its creation marks a collaborative effort within the Cloud Native Computing Foundation (CNCF) to standardize observability through a single, comprehensive framework.

OpenTelemetry aims to simplify the collection of metrics, logs, and traces across services and applications, offering developers and operators a unified approach to monitoring and troubleshooting.

Core Components of OpenTelemetry

OpenTelemetry consists of several key components that work together to facilitate end-to-end observability:

- **APIs and SDKs**: OpenTelemetry provides language-specific APIs and SDKs that enable the instrumentation of applications to capture telemetry data. These tools allow developers to embed observability into their code with minimal overhead.

- **Collectors**: The OpenTelemetry Collector acts as a centralized component that receives, processes, and exports telemetry data. It can be deployed as an agent within a host or as a stand-alone service, providing flexibility in how data is gathered and sent to analysis tools.

- **Exporters**: To accommodate the diverse ecosystem of observability tools, OpenTelemetry supports various exporters that enable telemetry data to be sent to different backends and platforms, such as Prometheus for metrics, Jaeger and Zipkin for traces, and ELK or Grafana Loki for logs.

The Significance of OpenTelemetry

OpenTelemetry's unified approach to collecting telemetry data significantly reduces the complexity and cost associated with observability. By providing a standardized way to gather and export data, it enables organizations to focus more on analyzing and deriving insights from their telemetry, rather than grappling with the intricacies of instrumentation. Furthermore, OpenTelemetry's commitment to openness and vendor neutrality ensures that it can be integrated into any observability stack, offering flexibility and future-proofing investments in monitoring tools.

OpenTelemetry and Enhanced Observability

The advent of OpenTelemetry represents a pivotal shift in observability strategies, emphasizing the importance of open standards and community-driven development. Its comprehensive framework not only streamlines the collection of telemetry data but also enhances the depth and breadth of observability across systems. With OpenTelemetry, teams can achieve a granular understanding of their software's performance and behavior, enabling proactive issue resolution, performance optimization, and ultimately, the delivery of better software experiences.

Leveraging Observability for Enhanced Security

Observability also plays a pivotal role in enhancing the security of software systems. By providing deep visibility into every aspect of the application, observability tools can detect unusual patterns or behaviors that may indicate a security threat. This visibility allows teams to respond to potential security incidents with speed and precision, mitigating risks and minimizing impact. Furthermore, the insights gained through observability practices can inform ongoing security strategies, helping to build more resilient systems.

Leveraging Service Mesh Framework for Full Observability

In today's microservices architecture, observability is crucial for maintaining system health, diagnosing issues, and ensuring smooth operation. Traditional methods of observability, which often rely on logging, metrics, and tracing, can fall short when dealing with the complexity and dynamism of microservices. In the previous section, we explored the OpenTelemetry framework, which greatly facilitates observability implementation but still requires setting up individual components. Introducing a service mesh framework takes observability a step further toward out-of-the-box automation, enabling a fully implemented observability solution.

Understanding Service Mesh

A service mesh is an infrastructure layer that enables managed, observable, and secure communication between microservices (Figure 7-3). It operates transparently to the application, allowing developers to focus on business logic while the service mesh handles inter-service communication, security policies, and observability.

185

The core component of a service mesh is the sidecar proxy, deployed alongside each microservice instance. These proxies intercept and manage all network traffic between services, providing a centralized control point for routing, security, and observability.

Key Observability Components in a Service Mesh

A service mesh framework typically provides several key observability components:

- **Distributed Tracing**: Service mesh frameworks like Istio and Linkerd support distributed tracing out of the box. They integrate with tracing tools such as Jaeger or Zipkin, capturing detailed trace information for every request that flows through the system. This allows developers to visualize request paths, measure latency, and identify bottlenecks. Distributed tracing helps in pinpointing where in the process delays or errors occur, providing a detailed map of the interactions between services.

- **Metrics**: The sidecar proxies collect and export a rich set of metrics related to service performance, resource utilization, and error rates. These metrics are often integrated with monitoring systems like Prometheus, enabling real-time monitoring and alerting. Metrics such as request counts, latency, error rates, and resource usage provide a quantitative measure of the system's performance and health.

- **Logging**: Service meshes provide enhanced logging capabilities, aggregating logs from all services and proxies. This centralized logging approach simplifies log management and analysis, making it easier to detect and diagnose issues. Centralized logging ensures that logs are consistent, easily accessible, and analyzable across the entire microservices ecosystem.

- **Traffic Management and Visualization**: A service mesh allows for fine-grained control over traffic routing and load balancing, which can be monitored and adjusted in real time. Visual tools integrated with the service mesh can display traffic flows, service dependencies, and health statuses, providing a clear picture of the system's behavior.

- **Security Observability**: Service meshes often include built-in security features such as mutual TLS, which also produce observability data. This includes information about authentication, authorization, and encryption status, helping to ensure that security policies are being enforced correctly and that any anomalies are quickly identified.

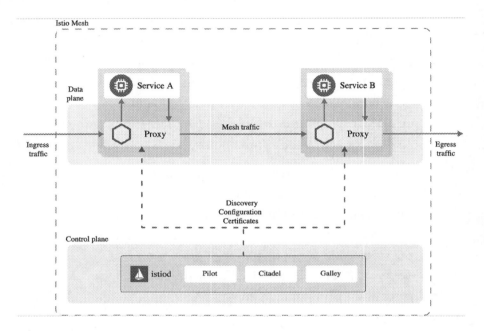

Figure 7-3. *Istio Service mesh architecture*

Benefits of Service Mesh Observability

Implementing observability through a service mesh framework offers several advantages:

- **Unified Observability**: With a service mesh, observability is unified across all services and layers of the stack, providing a single pane of glass for monitoring and troubleshooting. This holistic view simplifies the process of understanding system behavior and identifying issues.

- **Reduced Complexity**: The service mesh abstracts the complexity of observability away from the application code, reducing the burden on developers and ensuring consistent observability across the system. Developers can focus on business logic, while the service mesh handles observability concerns.

- **Enhanced Security**: Observability features in service meshes often include security-related metrics and logs, aiding in the detection of security incidents and policy violations. By monitoring security-related data, organizations can quickly respond to potential threats and enforce compliance with security policies.

- **Scalability**: Service meshes are designed to handle the high volume and dynamic nature of microservice environments, scaling observability efforts seamlessly as the system grows. As new services are added or existing ones are scaled up, the service mesh continues to provide comprehensive observability without additional configuration.

- **Operational Efficiency**: Automated observability provided by a service mesh reduces the manual effort required to set up and maintain observability tools. This efficiency translates to faster deployment times, quicker incident resolution, and lower operational costs.

By leveraging a service mesh framework, organizations can achieve comprehensive observability with minimal effort, enhancing their ability to maintain and operate complex microservices architectures effectively. This automated, out-of-the-box approach simplifies observability, making it a critical component of modern microservices deployments. The integration of distributed tracing, metrics, logging, traffic management, and security observability within a single framework ensures that all aspects of system behavior are monitored, understood, and optimized.

Conclusion

As we conclude our exploration of software observability, it's clear that observability is not just a technical requirement but a strategic asset in managing and maintaining modern software systems. This chapter has delved into the essential components and best practices of observability, providing a comprehensive understanding of its importance and implementation.

Key Takeaways

- **The Three Pillars of Observability**: The foundation of effective observability lies in the three pillars: logs, metrics, and traces. These pillars work together to provide a complete picture of the system's behavior and performance, enabling teams to detect and diagnose issues efficiently.

- **Observability vs. Monitoring**: While monitoring involves keeping a watchful eye on known issues and system metrics, observability goes a step further by providing insights into unknown issues and complex system behaviors. Understanding this distinction is crucial for building resilient systems.

- **Embracing OpenTelemetry**: OpenTelemetry has emerged as a unified framework for observability, simplifying the integration of observability tools and providing a standardized approach to collecting, processing, and exporting telemetry data. Its significance lies in enhancing the observability capabilities across different platforms and services.

- **Leveraging Observability for Enhanced Security**: Observability is not just about performance and reliability; it also plays a critical role in security. By leveraging detailed logs, metrics, and traces, teams can detect unusual activities, identify potential security breaches, and respond promptly.

- **Strategic Logging Practices**: Effective logging is essential for observability. Understanding log levels and implementing best practices for logging ensures that logs are meaningful, actionable, and not overwhelming. Centralizing log management further enhances the ability to monitor and analyze logs across the entire system.

- **Leveraging Service Mesh for Full Observability**: Integrating observability within a service mesh framework takes observability a step further toward out-of-the-box automation, enabling a fully implemented observability solution.

Software observability is a critical component of modern software engineering, providing the insights needed to maintain high-performing, secure, and resilient systems. By embracing the principles and practices of observability, such as implementing the three pillars, utilizing OpenTelemetry, and adopting strategic logging practices, teams can gain a deeper understanding of their systems and proactively address issues before they impact users. Observability transforms unknowns into knowns, equipping teams with the tools to build and maintain robust software in an increasingly complex digital landscape.

CHAPTER 8

Bridging the Gap Between Technology and Business

As we approach the final chapter of our exploration into the multifaceted world of software development, it is crucial to recognize that mastering the technical aspects, while essential, is only one part of the equation. This chapter, though last, is by no means the least important. It is here that we delve into the critical business skills that tech leaders need to effectively navigate the software product development landscape, ensuring that their teams are not just efficient but also aligned with broader business objectives.

The journey of transforming a concept into a successful software product is intricate, requiring a delicate balance between technological innovation and strategic business planning. Understanding the Software Product Development Life Cycle is paramount, as it offers a roadmap for turning ideas into viable products. Within this framework, concepts such as the Minimum Viable Product (MVP) and the Lean Startup methodology provide practical approaches for rapid, feedback-driven development, emphasizing the importance of learning and iterating quickly in response to market demands.

© The Editor(s) (if applicable) and The Author(s),
under exclusive license to APress Media, LLC, part of Springer Nature 2024
A. Souza, *Tech Leadership Playbook*, https://doi.org/10.1007/979-8-8688-0543-1_8

Moreover, the concept of the Cost of Delay highlights the critical nature of timing in product development, urging leaders to weigh the potential impacts of postponing features or decisions. This introduces a strategic dimension to decision-making, where understanding the trade-offs between building a solution in-house, acquiring existing solutions, or outsourcing development becomes essential. Each option carries its implications for control, cost, speed, and quality, demanding a careful evaluation to align with the company's goals and capabilities.

In addition, we will explore the strategic consideration of in-house development vs. outsourcing, a decision that can significantly influence the trajectory of product development. Factors such as core competencies, resource availability, and market responsiveness play a crucial role in this determination, shaping the path to product realization.

Finally, the chapter will touch upon the significance of the Net Promoter Score (NPS) as a measure of customer satisfaction and loyalty. Understanding and leveraging NPS can provide invaluable insights into the perceived value of your product, guiding continuous improvement and fostering a customer-centric development culture.

This chapter aims to equip tech leaders with the business acumen necessary to steer their projects toward success in a competitive landscape. By integrating business strategies with technical excellence, leaders can ensure that their teams not only create innovative software solutions but also contribute to achieving the company's strategic goals. The intersection of technology and business is where truly impactful software products are born, and mastering this domain is essential for any tech leader aspiring to make a significant mark in the industry.

The Software Product Development Life Cycle: A Guide for Tech Leaders

Understanding the Software Product Development Lifecycle from its inception is an essential competency for tech leadership. It ensures that technological efforts are not only aligned with business strategies but also directly contribute to fulfilling market needs and delivering value to customers. This life cycle spans several phases, each critical to the transition from a business concept to a successful software product in the market.

Phase 1: Conception and Market Research

The genesis of a software product lies in thorough market research. This initial phase is foundational, involving the identification of market needs, understanding the competitive landscape, customer persona analysis, and budget allocation for developing a Minimum Viable Product (MVP). Knowing who your competitors are and what your target users expect from such a product is crucial. This phase ensures that the product concept is viable, desirable, and feasible before any development begins. The outcome of this phase is a well-defined business case and a strategic plan for the MVP that addresses specific market gaps or user needs.

Phase 2: High-Level Design and Prototyping

With a solid understanding of the market and a clear vision for the product, the next step is to translate this vision into a tangible design. Phase 2 focuses on the high-level design and prototyping of the software solution. This involves outlining the main components of the software, their interactions, and how they fit into the overall system architecture. Prototyping plays a vital role here, offering a preliminary visual and functional representation of the product, which can be used to validate concepts, gather early feedback, and refine the product's design. This phase bridges the gap between conceptual planning and detailed development, setting the stage for actual software creation.

Phase 3: Software Development

Phase 3 marks the transition from planning to execution. The actual software development begins, guided by the insights and frameworks established in the earlier phases. This stage involves detailed coding, continuous testing, and iterative feedback incorporation to ensure that the software not only meets the predefined requirements but also adheres to quality standards. Agile methodologies often dominate this phase, emphasizing flexibility, customer feedback, and rapid iterations to adapt to changing requirements or new insights.

Phase 4: Release to Market and Maintenance

The final phase involves launching the software product into the market and entering into a cycle of ongoing maintenance and enhancement. This stage is critical for the product's success and includes marketing efforts, user education, and support systems. Post-launch, the focus shifts to monitoring the product's performance, gathering user feedback, and implementing necessary updates or patches. Maintenance is an ongoing process, aimed at keeping the software relevant, competitive, and aligned with user expectations.

The Software Product Development Life Cycle is a holistic journey that requires meticulous planning, strategic alignment, and agile execution. For tech leaders, mastering this life cycle means going beyond the confines of technical management to embrace a broader vision that integrates business strategy, market understanding, and user-centric design. By guiding their teams through these phases with a clear focus on market needs and product value, tech leaders can ensure the development of software products that are not only technologically advanced but also commercially successful and widely adopted.

The Strategic Imperative of the Minimum Viable Product (MVP)

In the dynamic arena of software development, the concept of the Minimum Viable Product (MVP) has emerged as a pivotal strategy for startups and established companies alike. The MVP approach is grounded in the philosophy of lean startup methodology, emphasizing the importance of speed, efficiency, and direct feedback in the product development cycle. This section explores the essence of an MVP, its benefits, and its role in validating business ideas in the most resource-efficient manner possible.

A Minimum Viable Product is the most basic version of a product that can be released with a minimal set of features that are enough to attract early-adopter customers and validate a product idea early in the product development cycle. The primary objective of an MVP is to learn about customers' problems and needs with the least effort, reducing the time and resources spent on products that do not meet market demands.

The rationale behind creating an MVP lies in its power to

- **Test hypotheses and validate assumptions** about the product's value proposition and customer needs with real users, in the real market, with the minimum effort and investment.

- **Gather and incorporate user feedback** quickly to iterate and improve the product, aligning more closely with market requirements and user expectations.

197

- **Reduce time to market** by focusing on core functionalities that solve specific problems, thus gaining a competitive advantage.

- **Minimize risks** and investment by avoiding the development of non-essential features that do not contribute to the product's primary value proposition.

An effective MVP should focus on the following key components:

- **Core Features**: Identify and include only the essential features that address the primary problem the product aims to solve for its target users.

- **User Experience (UX)**: Even with minimal features, ensuring a positive and intuitive user experience is crucial for engaging early adopters.

- **Feedback Loops**: Establish mechanisms to collect, analyze, and act on feedback from the initial users to inform future development cycles.

Creating an MVP requires a strategic approach that includes:

- **Market Research**: Understand the target market, customer pain points, and competitive landscape to inform the MVP's value proposition.

- **Feature Selection**: Prioritize features based on their ability to solve core customer problems and test key assumptions.

- **Build and Launch**: Develop the MVP focusing on simplicity and speed to launch. Use agile development methodologies to remain flexible and responsive to changes.

- **Learn and Iterate**: Collect user feedback rigorously and be prepared to iterate on the product. Use data-driven insights to make informed decisions about which features to add, modify, or remove in subsequent versions.

The Minimum Viable Product is not merely a stripped-down version of a software product; it's a strategic tool for learning and growth. By focusing on core functionalities and leveraging early user feedback, businesses can refine their offerings and align more closely with market needs. The MVP approach champions the idea of "fail fast, learn fast," enabling teams to discover the most viable path to product success with minimized risk and optimized resource utilization. In the journey of software product development, mastering the art of the MVP is essential for any tech leader aiming to bring innovative, market-fit products to life.

Embracing the Lean Startup Methodology

In the evolving landscape of startup development, the Lean Startup methodology has emerged as a transformative approach, fundamentally altering how new businesses are built and launched. Rooted in principles of lean manufacturing and adapted for the startup ecosystem, this methodology champions agility, customer feedback, and iterative design to create more sustainable business models. This section delves into the core tenets of the Lean Startup methodology, its application in software development, and its impact on fostering innovation and reducing market risks.

Developed by entrepreneur and author Eric Ries, the Lean Startup methodology synthesizes key concepts from agile development, customer-centric design, and lean manufacturing principles. It addresses the high failure rate among startups by proposing a systematic, scientific approach to creating and managing successful startups in an age characterized by rapid technological change and uncertainty.

The Lean Startup methodology is built around several key principles designed to guide startups through the uncertain terrain of launching a new business:

- **Build-Measure-Learn**: At the heart of the Lean Startup is the Build-Measure-Learn feedback loop. Startups begin by building a Minimum Viable Product (MVP) to test their hypotheses about the market and customer needs. They then measure the effectiveness of this MVP through customer feedback and learn from the results, informing the next cycle of development.

- **Validated Learning**: Rather than focusing solely on traditional metrics of success such as profit and scale, the Lean Startup methodology emphasizes validated learning—gaining insights into customer needs and behaviors that can steer the product toward real market demand.

- **Innovative Accounting**: This principle advocates for measuring progress, setting up milestones, and prioritizing work that contributes directly to learning about customers and meeting their needs.

- **Pivoting or Persevering**: Based on feedback and insights gained from the Build-Measure-Learn loop, startups must decide whether to pivot (make a fundamental change to their product strategy) or persevere (continue on their current course).

In the context of software development, the Lean Startup methodology encourages rapid prototyping, continuous user feedback, and frequent iterations. By integrating these practices, development teams can avoid extensive upfront planning and instead focus on creating products that closely align with user demands and market realities. This iterative process not only accelerates product development but also significantly reduces the cost and risk associated with launching new software.

The adoption of the Lean Startup methodology has profound implications for innovation within the tech industry. By fostering a culture of experimentation and adaptability, it allows startups to navigate the complexities of the market more effectively. The emphasis on customer feedback ensures that product development is continuously aligned with user needs, increasing the likelihood of achieving product-market fit.

Navigating the Cost of Delay in Software Product Development

In the competitive landscape of software development, time is not just a resource; it's a currency. The Cost of Delay (CoD) is a critical concept that quantifies the economic impact of time on the success of software products. Understanding and managing the Cost of Delay is essential for tech leaders who aim to optimize product delivery timelines without compromising quality or market fit. This section delves into the intricacies of Cost of Delay, its implications for decision-making, and strategies to mitigate its impact.

Cost of Delay combines an understanding of value with how time affects that value. It is the total financial impact incurred by delaying the launch of a software product or feature. CoD is not merely about the direct loss of revenue from postponed sales; it encompasses broader implications, including lost market opportunities, diminished competitive advantage, and the indirect costs of delayed feedback and learning.

Ignoring the cost of delay can have significant repercussions for software projects:

- **Missed Market Opportunities**: Delaying product launch can result in missing critical market windows or allowing competitors to capture market share first.

- **Reduced Product Value**: Products or features become less valuable over time as customer needs evolve and competitors fill the gap.

- **Compounded Development Costs**: Delays often lead to longer development cycles, increasing labor and operational costs.

- **Diminished Return on Investment**: The longer a product takes to reach the market, the shorter its life cycle for recouping investment and generating profit.

Calculating CoD involves assessing potential revenue, market share, or competitive advantage lost per unit of time. It requires a thorough understanding of the market, customer demand, and the financial metrics associated with the software product. While exact calculations can be complex and situation-dependent, even rough estimates can provide valuable insights for prioritizing development efforts.

Strategies to Mitigate Cost of Delay

- **Prioritize Based on Economic Impact**: Use CoD as a criterion for prioritizing features, projects, or initiatives. Focus on delivering the most value-driving elements first.

- **Adopt Lean and Agile Methodologies**: Implementing lean and agile development practices can shorten feedback loops, accelerate learning, and reduce time-to-market.

- **Continuous Deployment**: Embrace continuous deployment practices to reduce the lead time for getting features to users.

- **Cross-Functional Teams**: Foster collaboration among cross-functional teams to streamline decision-making and reduce bottlenecks in the development process.

- **Risk Management**: Proactively identify and mitigate risks that could lead to delays, applying strategies such as risk buffering and contingency planning.

The Cost of Delay is a powerful concept that underscores the economic significance of time in software product development. By understanding and actively managing CoD, tech leaders can make informed decisions that optimize the balance between speed, quality, and functionality. Integrating considerations of CoD into the strategic planning and execution of software projects not only accelerates value delivery but also enhances the overall competitiveness and financial performance of the product. In an industry where time-to-market can dictate success or failure, mastering the management of Cost of Delay is indispensable for any organization striving to lead in the digital age.

In-House vs. Outsourcing Software Development

In the dynamic realm of software development, one strategic decision that continually confronts tech leaders is whether to develop software in-house or to outsource it. This choice is not merely operational; it's foundational, with long-term implications for innovation, cost efficiency, and market competitiveness. This section explores the nuanced factors involved in making this critical decision, aiming to provide leaders with a framework for choosing the path that best aligns with their organizational goals and capabilities.

In-House Development refers to software creation by an organization's internal team, leveraging the company's resources, culture, and direct oversight. Outsourcing, on the other hand, involves hiring external entities—be it freelancers, agencies, or specialized firms—to handle the software development process.

Advantages of In-House Development

- **Alignment with Company Culture and Goals**: In-house teams are inherently aligned with the company's culture and long-term objectives, facilitating smoother collaboration and communication.

- **Direct Control and Oversight**: Tech leaders have direct control over the development process, allowing for agile responses to changes and closer management of project quality and timelines.

- **Intellectual Property Security**: Keeping development in-house can provide stronger safeguards for proprietary information and intellectual property.

- **Team Development and Retention**: Developing software in-house contributes to team growth, skill development, and higher employee engagement by investing in challenging and meaningful projects.

Challenges of In-House Development

- **Resource and Talent Constraints**: Building and maintaining a skilled in-house team requires significant investment in recruitment, training, and retention efforts, which can be particularly challenging in competitive talent markets.

- **Scalability Limitations**: Rapid scaling up for large projects can be difficult with in-house resources, potentially leading to bottlenecks and delays.

Advantages of Outsourcing Development

- **Cost Efficiency**: Outsourcing can offer cost savings, especially for short-term projects or where there is a significant difference in labour costs between regions.

- **Access to Global Talent and Expertise**: Outsourcing opens up a world of global talent, allowing companies to find specialized skills and expertise that might be scarce or too expensive locally.

- **Scalability and Flexibility**: External teams can be scaled up or down based on project needs, offering flexibility without the overhead of hiring or layoffs.

- **Focus on Core Competencies**: By outsourcing software development, companies can free up internal resources to focus on their core business areas and strategic initiatives.

Challenges of Outsourcing Development

- **Communication and Cultural Barriers**: Working with external teams, especially across time zones, can introduce challenges in communication and project alignment.

- **Quality Control and Oversight**: Ensuring the quality of the delivered software can be more challenging when the development process is not directly observed or managed.

- **Intellectual Property Risks**: Outsourcing introduces risks related to intellectual property security and requires careful contractual and operational safeguards.

Making the Decision

The choice between in-house and outsourcing software development depends on multiple factors, including project scope, budget constraints, available talent, strategic importance, and intellectual property considerations.

Tech leaders must weigh these factors carefully:

- **Evaluate Strategic Alignment**: Determine how the project aligns with the company's strategic goals and whether in-house or outsourced development better supports these objectives.

- **Consider the Total Cost of Ownership**: Beyond upfront costs, consider the long-term implications for maintenance, scalability, and team development.

- **Assess Risks and Mitigation Strategies**: Analyze potential risks associated with each approach and plan for how to mitigate them effectively.

The decision to develop software in-house or outsource it is a strategic one, with far-reaching consequences for innovation, operational efficiency, and market positioning. By carefully considering the advantages and challenges of each option, tech leaders can chart a path that not only meets the immediate needs of their software projects but also aligns with the broader vision and values of their organization.

The Net Promoter Score (NPS): Measuring Customer Satisfaction and Loyalty

The Net Promoter Score (NPS), is the measure that reflects how well the alignment of technology and business resonates with the end user.

Developed by Fred Reichheld, Bain & Company, and Satmetrix Systems in 2003, NPS is calculated based on responses to a single question: "On a scale of 0 to 10, how likely are you to recommend our company/product/service to a friend or colleague?" Based on their rating, customers are categorized as Promoters (score 9–10), Passives (score 7–8), or Detractors (score 0–6). The NPS is then calculated by subtracting the percentage of Detractors from the percentage of Promoters.

Importance of NPS

- **Customer Feedback**: NPS is more than just a number; it's direct feedback from customers that can reveal insights into their experiences and expectations.

- **Predictor of Growth**: High NPS scores are often correlated with word-of-mouth referrals, which can be a strong predictor of organic growth.

207

- **Competitive Benchmark**: NPS serves as a benchmark to compare against competitors and industry standards, allowing a business to gauge its standing in customer loyalty.

- **Focus on Customer Loyalty**: Unlike other metrics that might emphasize satisfaction at a single touchpoint, NPS reflects the overall loyalty and enthusiasm of customers, which is crucial for long-term success.

- **Driver for Improvement**: The simplicity of the NPS system allows for quick and clear identification of areas in need of improvement, driving companies to initiate targeted actions to enhance the customer experience.

Leveraging NPS for Business Transformation

To harness the full potential of NPS, businesses must

- **Act on the Feedback**: Collecting NPS data is just the start. The critical step is to analyze the feedback and implement changes to transform the customer experience.

- **Engage with Respondents**: Follow up with both Promoters and Detractors to understand their scores and build stronger relationships through personalized interactions.

- **Close the Loop:** Ensure that feedback leads to action. Let customers know that their voices have been heard and what steps are being taken as a result.

- **Integrate with Other Metrics**: Combine NPS with other customer metrics for a multidimensional view of customer experience and satisfaction.

In conclusion, the Net Promoter Score is a potent indicator of customer perception and a catalyst for business growth. It is a straightforward yet powerful tool that encapsulates the essence of customer loyalty and provides actionable insights. By diligently tracking and responding to NPS, companies can nurture a loyal customer base, refine their product offerings, and ultimately drive business success. The importance of NPS in today's business environment cannot be overstated—it is not just a score but a reflection of a company's relationship with its customers and a beacon guiding the journey toward exceptional customer service.

Conclusion

As we conclude this chapter on Technology and Business Alignment, it is clear that the journey of bringing a software product to life is as complex as it is rewarding. This convergence of domains demands a seamless blend of tech-centric innovation with business acumen—a duality that today's tech leaders must navigate with precision and foresight.

We have traversed the Software Product Development Life Cycle, understanding its critical phases from conception and market research to design, development, and market release. Each phase represents a step in a dance between technology capabilities and market needs, underscoring the importance of alignment at every juncture.

The concept of the Minimum Viable Product (MVP) and the embrace of the Lean Startup Methodology spotlight the necessity of agility and customer-focused innovation in today's fast-paced markets. By validating learning and iterating rapidly, tech leaders can steer their teams through the uncertainties inherent in software development.

The specter of Cost of Delay looms over every project decision, reminding us that timing is a strategic variable, not just a tactical one. The strategies to mitigate this cost—whether through prioritizing development, refining processes, or understanding when to release—are critical to maintaining competitive edge and market relevance.

The decision between in-house and outsourcing development presents a strategic fork in the road, each path laden with its unique benefits and challenges. This decision, much like every other examined in this chapter, is not about finding a universal answer but about finding the right fit for your organizational goals, culture, and the specific challenges at hand.

The Net Promoter Score (NPS), the final piece of our exploration, is the measure that reflects how well the alignment of technology and business resonates with the end user. It is a litmus test for customer satisfaction and loyalty, and a compass for continuous improvement.

As we close this chapter, let's carry forward the understanding that technology and business alignment is the heartbeat of successful software development—a rhythm that pulses through every strategy, decision, and innovation.

Index

A

Agile estimation and planning
  backlog management, 52
  in hours, 52, 53, 56
  metrics, 56, 57
  project, 52
  purpose, 56
  Scrum velocity with
    caution, 55, 57
  story points, advantages, 53, 54
  story points value, 57
  team happiness *vs.* velocity, 55
  user stories, 51

Agile estimation techniques, 62

Agile Manifesto, modern software
  development
  frequent feedback loops, 34, 35
  iterative development and
    continuous delivery, 34
  principles, 33
  values, 32, 33
  in 2001, 32

Agile meetings, 62
  Agile project management, 60
  Agile teams, 60
  backlog refinement
    meetings, 58

daily stand-up meetings, 58
  practices, 59, 60
  sprint planning meetings, 59
  sprint review meetings, 59

Agile principles, 20, 29, 31, 35, 53,
  55–57, 61, 156

Agile project management
  nutshell, 30, 31
  processes and decisions, 30
  team workflow (*see* Team
    workflow)

Agile Software Project
  Management, 30–31

API gateways, 113

Architectural principles, 87,
  104, 123

Architectural styles, 124
  microservices (*see* Microservice
    architecture)
  monoliths, 115

Architecture testing, 123
  adherence to architectural
    principles, 104
  enforcing component
    boundaries, 104
  non-functional testing, 104
  preserving system design, 104

Printed in the United States
by Baker & Taylor Publisher Services